"A book that is sure to stick, *Wear Clean Underwear* is part story, part education, and pure brilliance!"

Michael Gerber, father, bestselling author of *The E-Myth Revisited* and *Awakening the Entrepreneur Within*, and chief dreamer at www.IntheDreamingRoom.com

"I wish my family had read this book! Even though we employed the 'top experts' in estate planning, my mother was mired in the painful four-year probate of my father's estate after his death. This could have been avoided had we known what Alexis shares in this book. EVERYONE needs to read it!"

Christine Comaford-Lynch, CEO and founder of Mighty Ventures and *New York Times* bestselling author of *Rules for Renegades: How to Make More Money, Rock Your Career, and Revel in Your Individuality*

"If you can't stand the thought of reading pages and pages of technical advice, but you desperately want to protect your child's future, this is the book for you."

Abigail Dotson, Healthy House Expert and mom, www.AbigailDotson.com

"If you want to leave your children financially and emotionally secure no matter what and never leave their welfare up to chance, *Wear Clean Underwear* is a must-read."

Michael Port, bestselling author of *Book Yourself Solid* and *Beyond Booked Solid*

"This book is a pleasure to read—not at all like most uptight, dry estate planning books. Alexis knows how to set up scenarios that connect with the reader. As a devoted mom myself, I couldn't put it down! Who knew estate planning could actually be enjoyable?"

Lorrie Morgan-Ferrero, mom, entrepreneur and founder of redyhotcopy.com

D0188105

"Before I read this book, just thinking about my son being left behind in the event of my and/or my husband's untimely death left me with sweaty palms and a pit in my stomach. I actually feel better now, knowing that we can create a Plan B for his short- and long-term care that puts his well-being in the hands of people we love and trust and whose values we share. I will be contacting a personal family lawyer as soon as possible to set up that plan."

Jenny Yerrick Martin, mom and founder/CEO of Momentum Personal Promotion

"*Wear Clean Underwear* is a must-read for busy parents who want the straight facts about must-do legal planning for their children."

Julie Hall, the Estate Lady®, author of *The Boomer Burden* and mom

"Alexis Martin Neely brings intelligence and wit with the requisite heart and passion to this essential guide book for parents. Her plain-speaking but never-boring approach makes it easy on the brain and the anti-thesis of what you'd expect from a top tier legal eagle. Parents: Put this on your list; you'll feel better about your kids' future (and your stealth ability to plan) after one informative paragraph."

Amy Swift, co-author, *Ladies Who Launch: Embracing Entrepreneurship and Creativity as a Lifestyle*, editor-in-chief, Ladies Who Launch, www.ladieswholaunch.com

"You know you should assign guardians. You know you should protect your assets. *Wear Clean Underwear* tells you the rest of the story."

Alicia Dunams, founder of Wealthy Girl Summit 2008 and author of *Goaldigger*

"As parents, we spend so much time and effort on how to prepare our children for the future, yet we often overlook the reality of how to protect and secure our children's future if we're no longer around. Using compelling stories, Alexis Neely reveals the critical steps parents must address to plan effectively for their children's future. An eye-opening and much needed guide!"

Carolyn Ellis, founder, ThriveAfterDivorce.com and author, *The 7 Pitfalls of Single Parenting: What to Avoid to Help Your Children Thrive after Divorce*

"*Wear Clean Underwear* is an easy-to-understand guide for parents who want to leave their children not just with financial security, but peace and guidance in case of any eventuality. By reading and applying the principles in the book, if the worst does happen, your family and friends will be left empowered instead of frustrated and confused. A must read!"

Elizabeth Potts Weinstein, CFP®, attorney, mom, author of *Grow Up! Strategies: The 7 Legal & Financial Strategies You Need to Up-Level Your Small Business* and host of The Wealth Spa Radio Show.

"The strategies in Alexis' book, *Wear Clean Underwear*, are essential reading for every parent. The wisdom in these pages has ensured the well-being of my entire family, especially my greatest source of joy…my daughter! Thank you for writing this much needed book."

Christine Kloser, author of *The Freedom Formula*, mom, and founder of the Conscious Business Circle

"Do you wish you could stop worrying about your children's future so you could spend more time enjoying the present? *Wear Clean Underwear* provides the peace of mind of knowing your children will be safe and loved no matter where you are."

Allana Pratt, mother, Number-one-rated radio host of *How Mama Got Her Groove Back* and founder of SexyMomTalks.com

"As a parent, you want to provide your children with love, support and protection through every age and stage of their lives, *Wear Clean Underwear* is the perfect parent guide to provide you the tools, tips and techniques to protect your most valuable asset – your family. And it does this in a fast, easy, and fun way!"

Sanyika Calloway Boyce, financial fitness coach and author of *Crack Da Code* and *Teen Money Tips*

"A rare and devoted book that understands and integrates the multidimensional emotional, personal, and legal challenges of estate planning."

Richard W. Newman, Ph.D., founder of FINANCIALife Planning

"Alexis Martin Neely is the authority on values-based estate planning for parents, and her book is about so much more than passing on financial assets: it's about love, values, family, and so much more."

Susan Solovic, CEO of SBTV.com and author of *The Girls' Guide to Building a Million-Dollar Business*

"*Wear Clean Underwear* is a must-read for parents who want to ensure their children's safety and happiness."

Shay Pausa, mother and founder of Chikii Woman to Woman

"*Wear Clean Underwear* will impact the way you think about your assets, values and children. Now is the time to take action; it could save your children from paying excessive estate taxes or suffering a drawn-out probate. More importantly, what you do today could ensure your values are passed down for generations; leave the legacy you intended to leave. Read *Wear Clean Underwear* today and get started."

Loral Langemeier, mother, master coach, wealth strategist, best-selling author of the *Millionaire Maker* book series: *The Millionaire Maker, The Millionaire Maker's Guide to Wealth Cycle Investing* and *The Millionaire Maker's Guide to Creating a Cash Machine*, and founder and CEO of the wealth building community LiveOutLoud.com

"I constantly drill into my students the importance of having a competent, ethical and honest personal family lawyer. This is an attorney who is an expert in your state laws who is willing to go the extra mile to get to know your family and special situation. Alexis Martin Neely is the personal family attorney who is taking this vital message to families nationwide. Her advice in this book is not just important, it's vital to the future of you and your children. I wish my father had read this book before his unexpected death and the resulting mess that was left behind, all of which could have been avoided had he known what Alexis teaches you here."

Dr. Scott Brown PhD, author of *The Wallet Doctor's Rock Solid Foundations of Investing*, www.WalletDoctor.com

"When it comes to the safety of your kids, what could happen after you are gone is as important as what happens during your lifetime; to know your kids would always be cared for by people you want, in the way you want. Alexis Martin Neely tackles this subject with easy-to-understand, parent-friendly language, and makes it simple for us to take action. Excellent – read this book!"

Pattie Fitzgerald, founder of Safely Ever After, Inc., www.safelyeverafter.com

"This book considers the complete realm of prosperity and wealth; it's not just money, it's what you do with your money and whether you use it to strengthen your values and provide a lasting legacy for your children."

Lori Mackey, founder of Prosperity4Kids, Inc, and author of *Money Mama & The Three Little Pigs*

"To be a great parent today, you've got to think about your kids' future after you are gone. *Wear Clean Underwear* makes it easy to do while giving you the tools you need to take the next steps."

Maryanne Comaroto, mother, author of *Skinny, Tan and Rich; Unveiling the Myth*, and relationship advocate on HealthyLife.net

"Parents: Read this guide before you spend another day away from your kids!"

WEAR CLEAN
Underwear!

A Fast, Fun, Friendly
- and Essential -
Guide to Legal Planning
for Busy Parents

Alexis Martin Neely

New York

Wear Clean Underwear!

By Alexis Martin Neely
© 2008 All rights reserved.

ISBN: 978-1-60037-441-8 (Paperback)
Library of Congress Control Number: 2008925226

Published by:

Morgan James Publishing, LLC
1225 Franklin Ave. Suite 325
Garden City, NY 11530-1693
800.485.4943
www.MorganJamesPublishing.com

Cover Design by:

Tony Laidig
www.thecoverexpert.com

Interior Design by:

Megan Johnson
Johnson2Design
www.Johnson2Design.com
megan@Johnson2Design.com

To Kaia and Noah, the loves of my life:
Without the two of you, I never would have embarked on this journey.
Thank you for sharing me.

Acknowledgments

I have always loved reading acknowledgments because of the corresponding insight I glean by the people the authors thank. One insight from reading all of those acknowledgments is this: a book does not get written or published without a whole team behind it. With the completion of my first book, I am thrilled to acknowledge the team that has contributed unending passion and countless hours to this book.

At the top of the list is my most wonderful editor, Jocelyn Baker, who came up with the idea to structure this book in the style of a *Choose Your Own Adventure* story and kept me moving forward. It took a long time, but we finally did it!

Immense gratitude goes to Family Wealth Planning Institute Executive Vice President Laura Lee Sparks, who took me out of the day-to-day tasks of running my business so I could focus on the big picture.

I am forever grateful to Susan Odle, Nathalie Saxen, and Bari Vallas, the Martin Neely & Associates team, for holding down the fort. And to Corey, the best personal assistant a girl could ever possibly ask for: thank you, thank you—a million times—thank you.

My sincerest gratitude to the whole Morgan James team for seeing the possibilities, and to my amazing public relations team—Alicia Dunams, Brian Feinblum, and Stacie Krajchir, most notably—all of whom helped spread the word about the critical information contained in this book.

Judy Shannon: Without your insightful questions, the Kids Protection Plan may never have come to the light of day. You were the catalyst for answering this question: *what would happen to my children in the short term if I were in an accident?* Though I had thought much about the long term, I had never thought about this very critical question. Turns out no one else had either.

Thank you to all of the Ladies Who Launch for supporting my dream. You jumped in when I needed preview readers and jolts of creativity. And to "Auntie" Amy Finnigan of 96words.com, who came up with the perfect book title.

And to all the women who have helped me raise my kids and continue to do so - Martha, Joanne, Karinna, Abbe, Anna, Chelsey, and Jodi. I love you

Josh, Jose, and Kiehl from Everyangle Media: You are rock stars! Thanks for letting me push you far beyond what any of us thought was possible. And Tritia K., I never could have made everything so mommy-friendly without you.

To my two moms, one by birth and the other by my dad's good luck, Ronnie and Amy Martin: thanks for showing me how to love. And to Nan, my first best friend.

To the father of my babies, Todd Neely: You are a terrific daddy. I feel peace in my heart knowing that if anything did happen to me, Kaia and Noah would be taken care of so well by you.

Courtney Martin: You are the person I choose to raise my children should the need ever arise. I made this choice not because you are my sister, and not because you are the person who has known me the longest. You are my best friend, my confidante, and the person who knows me best of all, sometimes even better than I know myself.

And last, but as far from least as you can get, to my love, David Dee: Without your guidance and love, I'd still be trying to figure out how to get this message out to the world. You not only set me on the right path, but you also captured my mind and my heart. Thank you for supporting me so completely and giving me the confidence to follow my dream.

Contents

A Personal Message from Alexis Martin Neely — ix

Story One: Sara and Carlos—
Your Young Children and the Loves of Your Life — 1

Additional Resources: For Choosing the Right Guardians
and Legally Documenting Your Choices — 45

Story Two: Chelsea and Alex—
You Leave Behind Millions, but How Will Your Child
and Spouse Handle Life Without You? — 49

Additional Resources: For Choosing the Right Trustees
and Making Smart Financial Choices — 93

Story Three: You and Aiko—
Not a Lot of Assets, but a Whole Lot of Love — 95

Additional Resources: Making Life as Easy as Possible
for Your Loved Ones, Even if You Don't Have a Lot — 149

About the Author — 151

*T*he day my daughter was born, I became aware that a piece of me would live forever. It was no longer enough to wear clean underwear in case I ended up in the hospital; I needed to prepare a whole host of other things. Suddenly, I was a mom; I was responsible for my daughter's life and keenly aware that my choices could ripple through future generations.

In an easy-to-read story format, *Wear Clean Underwear* shows you how the preparations (or the lack thereof) you make today will impact generations to come, guiding you quickly and easily to do the right thing for the people you love most.

This book is about living the best life you can, leaving the world a better place and setting the foundation for the success of your spouse, children, and loved ones, no matter how long you live and no matter how much money you leave behind.

If you are anything like me, you do not want to think about dying. In the back of your mind, you secretly hope "they" find a cure for death before it is your time. But in truth, you have accepted that one day, you will die.

It is likely to be far in the future, when your kids are old and gray themselves, but no matter when it occurs, you can use the knowledge you learn by reading this book to focus on leaving the world a better place for your children and grandchildren.

Most of us have not planned at all for the time when we are not here. We plan for things that will likely never happen, like fires, hurricanes, and earthquakes. We plan for things that are not particularly important, like our trips to the grocery store or the hardware store. We spend an inordinate amount of time planning our children's birthday parties and play dates. So why do we fail to plan for something guaranteed to happen: our lives and eventual deaths?

Is it because we are too busy? Because we do not think we will die anytime soon? Or is it because we are scared?

Probably.

But as you will learn from this book, imagining what will happen if you do not plan is exponentially scarier. If you leave this Earth without specifically spelling out what you want to happen, the government will take matters into its own hands.

The government does not know your children. It does not know your spouse. And it wants as much of your money as possible.

In all truth, planning can be scary as well. Going to a lawyer's office and sorting through a whirlwind of legal terms like *probate, per stirpes, trustees, executors,* and *health care directives* is intimidating.

What if your lack of understanding leads you to the wrong choice? If you only understood the legalese, the choices might be easier.

Wear Clean Underwear: A Fast, Fun Friendly—and Essential—Guide to Legal Planning for Busy Parents not only boils down the complexities to simple, easy-to-understand terms, but also guides you through unique stories showing real examples of what would happen to your assets, children, spouse, or loved ones if you were in an accident, based on the choices you make now. You will then have the context for making crucial decisions about your life and your legacy.

This book is broken into three stories, each of which provides a layman's explanation of the legal issues surrounding planning for the care of your children and your money. Each story concludes with additional websites with checklists and free resources detailing the avenues available to you in your own family wealth planning.

Before we get started, let me explain one thing about a term you will see throughout this book: "family wealth."

To me, "estate planning" is an old, outdated term that does not apply to the kind of planning you are thinking about as a parent of young children. "Estate planning" suggests that you are planning merely for the passage of your assets (your estate) after you are gone.

But family wealth planning is about so much more than assets. Done right, family wealth planning prepares your children for a future without you, whether it is two weeks from now or fifty years from now. Family wealth planning requires you to decide proactively how you want to leave the world, intentionally focusing on what you can do in the here and now so that you can not only pass on your financial wealth, but also your values, insights, stories, and experiences, also known as your family wealth.

Family wealth planning is about your life, not your death.

Before we get started, here's a note about terminology and naming conventions. Each of these stories is written so that you can step into the role of the narrator and put yourself in the shoes of the decision-making parent. To the best of my ability, I have kept all names gender neutral so that the stories resonate regardless of whether you are a man or a woman or whether your parenting partner is a man or a woman.

In addition, for consistency and ease of reading, I have identified the person with whom you have children as your "spouse." In almost every case, the issues are identical whether a couple is unmarried or married.

If you are in an unmarried relationship, either by choice or because the law does not allow your marriage, please know that I respect your circumstances, and substitute the word "partner," "ex-spouse," "life partner," "baby-daddy," "baby-mama," or whatever other term you use, where appropriate.

Happy reading!

Alexis Martin Neely

STORY ONE:
Sara and Carlos

Your Young Children and the Loves of Your Life

Y ou and your spouse have created an amazing life together.

You love your son, Carlos, to distraction. He is kind, sensitive, helpful, and generous of spirit. He loves music, animals, and basketball. He warms your heart and makes you smile. You suspect he is a genius.

He cannot stand when you leave, not because he needs you, but because he loves helping you. When your daughter, Sara, was born, your love for Carlos grew exponentially. He calls Sara "his baby." He worries when she cries. "My baby is sad," he says, with tears in his eyes.

When pregnant with Sara, you and your spouse worried that you would not love her as much as you love Carlos. But your heart has expanded exponentially to accommodate your love for Sara, and even though she is different from Carlos in just about every way, you love her just as much as you love Carlos.

Sara has a mischievous sense of humor and wreaks havoc everywhere she goes. She earned the nickname "Hurricane Sara" by the time she was two. She makes you laugh. You suspect she is a genius.

You and your spouse are kind, loving, and attentive parents who make a great effort to be actively involved in your children's lives. They are your primary focus. Your spouse, who works for a prominent marketing firm, tries not to work more than eight hours a day, though business sometimes requires an out-of-town trip.

You are fortunate enough to work from home. Because your children are your first priority, you sometimes have difficulty finding time to work, especially with the constant interruptions.

To ease your burden a little, you and your spouse look for someone to help with child care and household errands. Because the two of you are financially successful, you can afford to be picky. Eventually, after searching for months and interviewing countless people with whom you would never leave your children, you find the perfect nanny and assistant. Though she is only twenty, Courtney is mature beyond her years and has the patience of a grandmother. You hire her to run errands and to care for Carlos and Sara when you need to meet with clients or are facing a looming deadline.

Courtney is wonderful. She plays games with your children, rarely loses her temper, and teaches Carlos and Sara to speak Spanish. Your children love her, and you trust her unconditionally.

One morning, you have a three-hour meeting with a client at his office. Your spouse is in France on business. On your way out the door, you remind Courtney to call your cell phone if she needs you, which you always leave on vibrate in case anything comes up.

When you arrive at the client's office, you learn that your meeting has been postponed, though no one bothered to notify you. You are irritated, of course, but you decide to make the most of the time and grab a quick workout.

You park your car in the gym's vast parking lot and remember that cell phones are not allowed inside. From the parking lot, you try to call Courtney, but you receive a busy signal. You wait a couple of minutes and try calling again. The phone is still busy. This surprises you, and you make a mental note to have Courtney call the phone company to find out why the second line is not ringing.

You make a choice. Courtney is responsible and can handle anything in the unlikely event that something unexpected happens while you spend an hour in the gym. You turn off your cell phone, stow it in your gym bag, and stash your bag in a locker. You tell yourself that after you warm up, you will sneak into the locker room and try to call Courtney again.

While jogging on the treadmill, you worry about the kids. You remind yourself to stop worrying. Courtney will be fine for a little while without you.

And then, the unexpected happens. An aneurysm in your brain that has lain dormant for years—unseen, hidden, waiting—explodes.

Later, the doctors explain that the aneurysm had nothing to do with the fact that you were working out. It was just a time bomb in your brain that could not have been prevented, even with prior knowledge. It could have happened anywhere: at the grocery store, in line at the bank, at home with your kids.

But it happened while you were at the gym, with your gym membership, driver's license, and all other forms of identification in an anonymous locker, your cell phone turned off, and your car a needle in a haystack in the gym's parking lot.

The gym calls 911 immediately, but without any means of identifying you, no one knows to call Courtney. By the time the paramedics arrive, you are gone. You never have a chance to tell anyone about your kids, or Courtney, or that your spouse is on a business trip in a foreign country.

When you don't return home by 3:00 PM, Courtney calls your cell phone, but the call is sent straight to voice mail. *The meeting must have been long,* Courtney thinks. Still, she worries a little bit. It isn't like you to turn off your phone, and you always call when you are going to be late.

Things happen, Courtney thinks. *I'm sure everything is fine.* She tries to be positive.

Two hours later, she is panicked. She has been calling your mobile phone every fifteen minutes. She calls your client, only to discover that the meeting was canceled. She tries calling your spouse's cell phone, but the electronic voice says that the phone is "out of the service area." Courtney starts calling your friends.

None of them have seen or heard from you. Courtney calls the local hospitals, but since she is not a relative, no one will give her any information.

Courtney tries to stay calm around Sara and Carlos. She feeds your children, and though she rarely lets them watch TV, she sends them to your bedroom to watch cartoons before making a phone call.

Does Courtney call the police, or does she call someone else?

If your babysitter calls the police, turn to page 5. If your babysitter calls someone else, turn to page 9.

Courtney Calls the Police

Because you and your spouse did not have any sort of plan in place for what Courtney should do if something like this happened, Courtney does not know that she should wait to call the police until your children are safely in the hands of someone who has clear authority to stay with them in the event of your absence.

When the police arrive, they question Courtney and ask if your family has any relatives in town. Courtney does not know of any. The police try locating an executive at your spouse's marketing firm, but by this time, the office is closed.

"We'll take over from here. You can go home," Officer Matzo finally tells Courtney after questioning her.

"What will happen to Carlos and Sara?" asks Courtney.

Officer Matzo lets Courtney know that Child Protective Services will be responsible for Carlos and Sara's care until the authorities locate you, your spouse, or another family member and run the necessary background checks.

Courtney volunteers to keep the children with her overnight, but the authorities do not know anything about her. Leaving Carlos and Sara in her care without any legal documentation giving her authority is a potential liability for the authorities.

"No, Ma'am. You have got to go home now. The kids will be fine," Officer Matzo says in response to Courtney's continued pleading for him to allow the children to remain in her care.

Courtney refuses to leave until Child Protective Services arrives. She packs overnight bags for your children and promises them that they will be back home the next morning. When the social worker from Child Protective Services arrives, four-year-old Sara begins sobbing. She clings to Courtney and refuses to let go. When the social worker tries to pry Sara's fingers away, Courtney and steady-tempered Carlos, now eleven years old, both begin crying.

"This is ridiculous!" Courtney tells Officer Matzo and the social worker. "The children want to stay with me, and I want them to stay with me. What is the problem?"

Officer Matzo explains that Courtney has no documented authority to stay with the children. Without such documentation, the police and Child Protective Services are legally responsible for the children. The officer and the social worker think Courtney is too young to care for young children overnight. And when the authorities run a background check on Courtney, they discover that when she was seventeen and at a party following her high school graduation, she was arrested for possession of alcohol.

"You need to leave, Ma'am," Officer Matzo tells Courtney forcefully. He says that he needs to focus on your whereabouts, and Courtney's refusal to leave is slowing down the investigation. Giving your children a final embrace, Courtney has no choice but to leave. As she pulls away, she watches your children climb into the social worker's car.

Officer Matzo calls the local hospitals and is able to confirm your death. He alerts the social worker, who tells your children that you are not coming home.

Because your spouse cannot be located, your children are put in the care of a foster family: Joe and Savannah Liardino. The Liardinos are kind, but they have four other foster children in their care, so they are not as attentive as they could be. Carlos and Sara are bewildered, terrified, heartbroken, and angry. Sara is too young to fully comprehend the situation and keeps asking about you. Carlos cries each time he tells his little sister you are not coming home.

"Why can't we stay with Gus and Patsy?" Sara asks Mrs. Liardino, referring to your dear friends and next-door neighbors, Gustavo and Patricia Garcia. "We always spend the night with Gus and Patsy when Mommy and Daddy are gone." In fact, the Garcias think of your children as family and would have known how to care for them, but they had not answered the door hours earlier when Courtney knocked, looking for you. In the absence of any written instructions from you, neither the police nor the social worker tried to reach the Garcias.

The Liardinos know nothing about the Garcias. They do not know that Patsy and Gus have two children who are friends with Carlos and Sara. They do not know that your children often have slumber parties with the Garcias' children. They do not know that Carlos and Sara love and trust Gus and Patsy and that the Garcias would happily provide an immediate support system during a crisis.

The police do not know any of this, because you never made a legal plan to tell them.

So instead of spending the first hours after your death embraced by a family they know and trust, your children are stuck with the Liardinos. The police are finally able to contact your spouse early the next morning, but bad weather delays flights out of Paris, and your spouse is unable to fly home for another forty-eight hours. In the meantime, your children have become increasingly terrified and withdrawn. They think they may never see your spouse or their home again and that they will be stuck with the Liardinos and their four foster brothers and sisters forever.

When your spouse finally arrives, Carlos is so angry that he is having difficulty functioning; Sara is petrified to the point of catatonia. The oldest foster child in the home has been terrorizing Sara. Carlos has tried to defend her, but the older boy is bigger and stronger, and the Liardinos are indifferent.

Your spouse, who is equally devastated, takes your children home and tries to comfort them while dealing with the burden of notifying family and friends and arranging for your funeral.

Your only living relative, your estranged brother, comes to the funeral with his wife. They sit alone, barely speak to your spouse, and leave without saying a word to your children.

After the funeral, your spouse enlists the help of a child therapist and calls on parishioners and clergymen for support. Eventually, your family begins to heal.

When Sara is seven and Carlos fourteen, your spouse begins dating again. You would have wanted this, but Carlos feels hurt and abandoned, as though your spouse is betraying your memory. Sara, on the other hand, is slowly forgetting about you. She was barely four when you died, so she has few memories of you.

Have you created a plan to make sure that you remain a presence in your children's lives, even after your death?

If so, turn to page 13. If not, turn to page 17.

Courtney Does Not Call the Police

You and your spouse have been thorough. When Carlos was born, you prepared a comprehensive Kids Protection Plan, which provides instructions to your children's babysitters, day-care providers, teachers, and school administrators, detailing the people to call in the event of an emergency. By providing these instructions, Carlos and Sara's caretakers (including Courtney) know not to call the police until your children are safely in the hands of someone who has clear authority to care for them in the event of your absence.

The first names on the list are your neighbors, Gustavo and Patricia Garcia. Patsy and Gus have two children who are friends with Carlos and Sara. In fact, your children often have sleepovers with the Garcias' children, Travis and Sherry.

Although the Garcias are at the park, Courtney has their cell phone number, which you posted on the refrigerator when Courtney was hired. They return home as soon as Courtney calls them. The Garcias know that your unexplained tardiness means something is wrong, and because you prepared, they know they need to take care of your children until you or your spouse is located.

Because you and your spouse were so prepared, Patsy has a copy of the document you signed giving her legal authority to care for your children temporarily in just this type of situation. With this in hand, she feels confident that your kids will not be taken into foster care when the police arrive.

Together, Courtney and Patsy call the police. The police are relieved to learn that the Garcias have documented legal authority to care for your children. Without such documentation, your children would most likely be taken into the custody of Child Protective Services and placed in a foster home until your spouse could be located.

Post instructions for your children's caregivers on your refrigerator and distribute copies to all daycare providers, babysitters, teachers, instructors, and school administrators. For forms and templates, visit:

www.KidsProtectionPlan.com.

During traumatic times, children are always better off with familiar friends or family members rather than strangers, no matter how safe and capable. Your forethought means that your children will remain with people you know, love, and trust while the police track down your spouse and investigate your disappearance.

The police call the local hospitals and discover you have died. They contact your spouse, but bad weather has delayed flights out of Paris for forty-eight hours. In the meantime, Patsy cares for your children. They are, of course, devastated and do not completely understand that you will not be coming back. But because they love and trust Patsy and Gus, they have an immediate support system.

When your spouse arrives and takes your children home, they begin the process of grieving.

Your spouse arranges for your funeral, calling on your friends for comfort. Your only living relative, your estranged brother, comes to the funeral with his wife. They sit alone, barely speak to your spouse, and leave without saying a word to your children.

After the funeral, your spouse enlists the help of a child therapist and calls on parishioners and clergymen for support. Eventually, your family begins to heal.

When Sara is seven and Carlos fourteen, your spouse begins dating again. You would have wanted this, but Carlos feels hurt and abandoned, as though your spouse is betraying your memory. Sara, on the other hand, is slowly forgetting about you. She was barely four when you died, so she has few memories of you.

Have you created a plan to make sure that you remain a presence in your children's lives, even after your death?

If so, turn to page 13. If not, turn to page 17.

Carry a card in your wallet listing the names and contact information of the temporary guardians or first responders you have chosen to care for your children.

You Left Written and Recorded Messages About Your Values, Insights, Stories, and Experiences for Your Children.

From the first time you felt Carlos kick inside your belly, you thought about the life lessons you wanted to teach him: the values, insights, stories, and experiences you wanted to share with him when the time was right. You began to keep a mental file of what you wanted him to learn; by the time Sara was born, the mental file was bulging.

The first time you spent a night away from Carlos and Sara, you realized that all of these life lessons were locked up in your mind and that if anything happened to you, Carlos and Sara would never benefit from your mental file. Your concerns resurfaced when Carlos was nine. You were aware of how many of his beliefs—beliefs you did not necessarily want him to have—were shaped by his schoolmates, TV, and teachers. You knew that your chance to infuse his mind with life lessons was quickly passing.

You convinced your spouse to spend a weekend discussing the life lessons you wanted your kids to learn. Together, you wrote several letters and recorded CDs to be given to your children at specified birthdays, graduations, engagements, and on other milestone days, like their wedding days and when they each became parents themselves. You knew that it was likely that you would be reading the letters with them on those special days; you felt peace knowing that they would hear these life lessons from you even if you were not alive.

Though thinking about death is never pleasant, this weekend helped you and your spouse reach clarity on the values, insights, stories, and experiences you wanted to pass along, knowing that you had a plan for passing on these values.

Both kids were growing so fast, and with a hectic day-to-day life, you realized how easily they could grow up without benefiting from all the important things locked in your head. Soon, they would be too wrapped up with friends to listen to your insights into life. After that, you and your spouse were much more conscious of taking the time and creating the energy to share your values, insights, stories, and experiences at age-appropriate intervals.

As it turned out, you could not be at Sara's wedding. But after her soon-to-be husband proposes, Sara is given a letter from you about love and commitment. In the letter, you quote Kahlil Gibran's touching poem, "On Marriage."

Sara incorporates this poem into her vows. She feels your spirit at her ceremony. And though she has few memories of you, she has been hearing your voice and reading your letters throughout her life. She knows you, and she feels your love.

> *. . . let there be spaces in your togetherness,*
>
> *And let the winds of the heavens dance between you . . .*
>
> *—Kahlil Gibran*

And when Carlos goes on his first date at the age of fourteen, your spouse gives him a letter from you. The letter speaks of the excitement of new romance and his responsibility to be an honest, thoughtful gentleman. Carlos begins to realize that you would have wanted your spouse to enjoy life with someone new and that he has been unfair. He finally recognizes that your spouse should be able to enjoy the same excitement without being blamed for betraying your memory.

Turn to page 19.

You Did Not Leave Written and Recorded Messages for Your Children.

From the first time you felt Carlos kick inside your belly, you thought about the life lessons you wanted to teach him: the values, insights, stories, and experiences you wanted to share with him when the time was right. You began to keep a mental file of what you wanted him to learn; by the time Sara was born, the mental file was bulging.

Many times you thought about spending a weekend with your spouse discussing the values, insights, stories, and experiences you wanted to share with your children, but life was so hectic that you never scheduled time to create a plan to transfer your values to your children. You figured you would share the lessons when the time was right.

Your children were more important to you than your own life. They were constantly on your mind, so it never occurred to you that *they* could forget *you*. Though your parents died when you were a young adult, you remembered them with vivid details.

Sara starts to forget about you within a few months of your death. Carlos will never forget you, but the older he gets, the less he feels he knows you, and the more he feels is missing.

During milestone occasions, he often wonders what you would have said. When your spouse begins dating, Carlos feels certain that you would have disapproved (even though you wouldn't have). When he struggles with a difficult career choice—whether to follow his heart and be poor forever or to follow the money—he wonders what you would have said (follow your heart). When his first child is born, he wonders what advice you would have shared with him (learn to laugh when the baby spits up on your new suit).

Sara does not wonder about you at all. After all, she never really knew you.

Turn to page 19.

Your Spouse

Your family is doing as well as can be expected. The marketing firm that employs your spouse provided a yearlong sabbatical after your death, and fortunately you had enough life insurance for your spouse to afford the time off. During this time, Sara started afternoon kindergarten, and the family moved closer to the children's school. By the time your spouse goes back to work, both of your children are in school.

Since your death, your spouse has been in constant "drive" mode—driving your children to school, doctor's appointments, lessons, and all of the other activities the two of you wanted your children to participate in. Courtney still helps around the house, but your spouse has double the responsibility and is chronically exhausted.

One day, while driving home from work with a friend in the car, your spouse falls asleep at the wheel. Awakened by a blaring horn and screeching tires, your spouse is alive for only a split second before running into a semitruck. Your spouse's friend in the passenger seat also dies immediately.

When your spouse fails to arrive to pick up your children, Patsy and Gus know what to do. They locate the documents giving them the legal authority to serve as temporary guardians of your children, and they call the police.

Everyone is shocked to learn that your spouse has died so soon after you. "What will happen to the children?" they ask.

Turn to page 21 if you named permanent guardians. Turn to page 39 if you did not name permanent guardians for your children.

You Named Guardians for Your Children.

You considered what would happen if both you and your spouse died. In fact, your parents had been together when they died. Your father was an airline pilot who also had a private pilot's license. Though he was an expert flier, the single-engine plane he was piloting could not handle the storm that arose unexpectedly while he and your mother were making the short flight from Los Angeles to Santa Barbara.

Because you understood that it was all too possible for children to lose both of their parents, you insisted that you and your spouse complete the paperwork to name permanent guardians.

If you had the guidance of a Personal Family Lawyer when preparing your guardian nomination, turn to page 23. If you did not have the guidance of a Personal Family Lawyer when preparing your guardian nomination, turn to page 33.

You Had Guidance from a Personal Family Lawyer when Preparing Your Guardian Nomination.

The whole experience of naming guardians for your kids was much easier than you had expected. You met with a Personal Family Lawyer who not only prepared the legal documents for you, but also counseled you to decide who should raise your kids, which was important for you because you and your spouse were not entirely sure whom to choose.

Other than your estranged brother, neither of you had any immediate family, and neither of you were close with your extended families. You were at a loss when it came to making a decision. Your Personal Family Lawyer helped you determine what was important to you when deciding who would raise your children. You knew that you wanted your children raised by a married couple. You knew that you wanted them raised in your own neighborhood. Additionally, because you and your spouse valued cultural experiences, you also wanted your children raised by guardians who valued world travel and, ideally, who spoke more than one language.

You carefully considered couples who fit these criteria, shared your spiritual values, and had similar parenting philosophies. Eventually, you decided on two couples that you both considered the most likely to raise your children in an environment similar to the one you would provide: Karl and Robin Couch, and Patricia and Gustavo Garcia.

The Couches, both teachers, are less affluent than the Garcias. They certainly do not have enough money to send your children to a private school, much less to travel the world extensively. But they share your religion and your parenting philosophy. In fact, you and your spouse had known Robin since college and always admired her values. Though you did not know Karl as well, you trusted that Robin would marry a man with similar convictions.

On the other hand, the Garcia children attend the same private school as your children, and they spend summer and Christmas vacations in South America. The whole family is trilingual. You and your spouse met Gus and Patsy years ago when you first moved into your neighborhood during college. They became more than neighbors: they became your best friends. You loved them both equally, and you trusted them unconditionally with your children.

*Having trouble determining who would make a good guardian for your kids? Download the **Choosing the Right Guardian** worksheet at:* **www.KidsProtectionPlan.com.**

Nevertheless, the values exercise you worked through with your Personal Family Lawyer helped you determine that your religious values were most important to you. Because they share your religious values, you decided to make Robin and Karl your first choices as guardians. You figured that with proper planning, you could leave behind enough money to have your children sent to private school and to earmark money for foreign travel.

In case something happened to Karl and Robin, you listed the Garcias as your second choice for guardians.

Sadly, something *did* happen to Robin. The friend in your spouse's car, the passenger who also died immediately, was Robin.

Unless you had specified otherwise, Karl, a man you have only known a short time and who was only chosen as a guardian by virtue of your friendship with his deceased wife, would have been the guardian of your children.

But fortunately, your Personal Family Lawyer helped you see that because you had only known Karl a short time and because you wanted a married couple to raise your children, you should craft your guardian nomination so that the Couches would only take guardianship if they could act together. If they could not, you wanted your children to be raised by the next couple on your list, Patsy and Gus Garcia.

Then your wishes became a bit confusing, but your Personal Family Lawyer helped you to reach clarity. If Patsy and Gus could not serve together because something happened to one of them or if they were divorced at the time of your death, you wanted Robin Couch to raise your children, even if she divorced (or was widowed), but only if she lived in California. If she did not live in California, your next choices were Ann and Michael Cohen, whom you knew would never leave California.

Here is what your guardian nomination looked like:

Nomination of Guardian

If a guardian of the Person is required for any minor child of mine, I nominate Robin and Karl Couch jointly, so long as they are married and living together, to serve as guardians.

Alternate Guardians of Person

If the above-nominated guardians are unwilling or unable to serve or continue as guardian of the Person of my minor children, then I nominate the following individuals to serve as guardians listed in preferred order and not serving jointly unless so specifically noted:

Patricia and Gustavo Garcia, serving jointly, so long as they are married and living together in the State of California; then

Robin Couch, serving alone, so long as she is living in the State of California; then

Ann and Michael Cohen, serving jointly, so long as they are married and living together in the State of California; then

Patricia Garcia, serving alone, so long as she is living in the State of California; then

Gustavo Garcia, serving alone, so long as he is living in the State of California; then

Robin Couch, serving alone; then

Patricia Garcia, serving alone; then

Gustavo Garcia, serving alone; then

Michael Cohen, serving alone; then

Ann Cohen, serving alone.

When you mentioned that you never wanted your brother to take guardianship of your children under any circumstances, your Personal Family Lawyer prepared a confidential document to include in your plan that would stop your brother from assuming guardianship of your children. The document would only be revealed if your brother and his wife tried to take custody of your kids. It stated that in your opinion, your brother's wife is emotionally and verbally abusive to her own children. Your brother neglects his family, working sixteen-hour days so that he can ignore the situation at home as his family spirals out of control. The confidential document clarified that no matter how much they indicated that they had changed their lives, your brother and his wife were not to be named guardians of your children under any circumstances.

Confidentially exclude those family members whom you would never want to take guardianship of your children. If these people challenge your choice of guardian, they will have little choice but to withdraw their challenge.

At the time of your spouse's car accident, your children are in the care of the Garcias, who call your Personal Family Lawyer. Your lawyer immediately locates your guardianship paperwork designating Robin and Karl Couch as your first choice of guardians. Because Robin has died, your attorney arranges for your next choices, the Garcias, to assume permanent guardianship of Carlos and Sara.

In the meantime, your brother learns of your spouse's death. Upon learning that your first choices, the Couches, are unable to serve, your brother and sister-in-law decide to challenge the Garcias' guardianship.

To prepare free legal documents and name guardians for your children, visit:

www.KidsProtectionPlan.com.

On paper, your brother and his family are picture-perfect. Your brother earns a large salary as the area's leading oncologist. They have a lovely home in a fantastic neighborhood. Your sister-in-law is a homemaker, an active member of the PTA, and a charming socialite who serves on the boards of several nonprofit organizations and volunteers much of her time to charity work. The couple appears to value education, and their children attend only the best schools.

In the absence of any instruction from you and your spouse to the contrary, the court would no doubt have given serious consideration to granting your brother and sister-in-law guardianship After all, the couple seems picture-perfect, and the court would have no way to know about your sister-in-law's constant screaming or your brother's sixteen-hour work days. The court would not know that their own children's self-esteem has been so trampled by their parents' poor parenting skills and negative home environment that the children have started to act out, choose the wrong friends, and make dangerous choices. The court would not know, for instance, that it would be sending Carlos and Sara to live in a home where the older children have already started to experiment with drugs and sexuality.

But luckily, with the guidance of your Personal Family Lawyer, you thought ahead. And when your Personal Family Lawyer produces the confidential document excluding your brother and his wife, they immediately withdraw their petition for guardianship. They are hurt, ashamed, and angry. But they have no choice but to withdraw their petition for guardianship or suffer the embarrassment when your attorney and the courts are forced to expose the reasons for their exclusion.

Your children are protected, and in accordance with your wishes, the Garcias become legal custodians of Carlos and Sara.

Patsy and Gus make exemplary parents. Gus is a musician, and he teaches Sara to play the guitar; he knows she wants to be a singer. He also notices Carlos's artistic gifts and enrolls your son in a weekend class for budding artists.

Patsy and Gus do everything you imagined they would. Because your Personal Family Lawyer impressed upon you the importance of leaving behind letters and recorded messages for your kids, Patsy and Gus have no question as to how you want your kids raised and the values, insights, stories, and experiences you

Write letters to or record videos for your guardians with detailed instructions as to how you want them to handle such matters as religion and spirituality, education, career, money, values, and the like. Clearly indicate the people you want to be involved in your children's lives, even in your absence. Visit **www.KidsProtectionPlan.com** *for ideas and templates.*

want your children to have. They even raise them with the religious values that were so important to you.

When Sara tells the Garcias that she wants to pursue her musical interests instead of attending a university, they smile and congratulate her, because they know from your letters exactly how you wanted them to handle this situation.

"Not many people know what they want to do at such a young age," Patsy says.

"I know of a great community college you can attend part-time. It has a phenomenal music department. You can take a general education course and a few music courses while still having time for music gigs," Gus says. "Can I set up an interview?"

And Carlos? With the support of Patsy and Gus, Carlos's church (your church) introduces him to several world aid organizations. He is able to fight injustice by volunteering his time and efforts to developing countries.

In short, Carlos and Sara become people you would have been proud to call your children.

The last thing they do before going to bed each night is listen to the CD you recorded years before when you met with your Personal Family Lawyer to plan for your life and your legacy. Sara and Carlos heard you and your spouse talk about the life lessons you hoped to pass on and the love you felt for them. Despite their despair at losing you, your children feel infinite peace and know that everything will work out as it was supposed to, and they feel the loving embrace of an energy greater than themselves.

Congratulations. Your choice to plan for your life and your legacy has the lasting impact of increasing your family wealth for generations to come. You have left the world a better place. Turn to page 45 for more information about creating a legacy for your family.

You Did Not Have the Guidance of a Personal Family Lawyer when Preparing Your Guardian Nomination.

You figured it could not be that difficult to name guardians for your children. You went online to a legal document service and downloaded the forms you would need.

But you were uncertain whom to name. Other than your estranged brother, neither you nor your spouse had any immediate family. Neither of you were close with your extended families. You were at a loss when it came to naming guardians.

One thing you knew for certain was that you didn't want your brother and his wife to take guardianship of your kids under any circumstances. From the outside, they look like a picture-perfect family, but your sister-in-law is emotionally and verbally abusive to her own children, screaming at them for the smallest infractions. Your brother ignores the situation. Instead, he works sixteen-hour days, neglecting his family as it spirals out of control.

You decided to name your closest friends, Karl and Robin Couch or Patricia and Gustavo Garcia.

The Couches, both teachers, are less affluent than the Garcias. They certainly do not have enough money to send your children to a private school, much less to travel the world extensively. But they share your religion and parenting philosophy. In fact, you and your spouse had known Robin since college and always admired her values. Though you did not know Karl as well, you trusted that Robin would marry a man with similar convictions.

On the other hand, the Garcia children attend the same private school as your children. They spend summer and Christmas vacations in South America. The whole family is trilingual. You and your spouse met Gus and Patsy years ago when you first moved into your neighborhood during college. They became more than neighbors: they became your best friends. You loved them both equally and trusted them unconditionally with your children.

Nevertheless, because they share your religious values, you decided to make Robin and Karl your first choices as guardians. You figured that with proper planning, you could leave behind enough money to have your children sent to private school and to earmark money for foreign travel.

When you and your spouse were discussing potential guardians for your children, you both agreed that if possible, you wanted a married couple to raise your children. Though you had known Karl for only a short time, you trusted Robin enough to know that she would marry a kind, decent man with strong values. The couple was newly married and head over heels in love. *They'll never divorce*, you thought. But even if they did, you figured you would have time to update your guardianship paperwork to reflect that you would prefer Patsy and Gus Garcia to raise your children.

You never considered what would happen if one of them died. You should have. You spent a lot of time with Robin, and you should have considered the possibility that she might be with you if you died in an accident.

But you did not consider those things. Frankly, you just did not know about everything you should consider when creating the forms. Instead, you followed the online instructions, which did not suggest an individualized consultation with a lawyer trained to help you think through in-depth issues.

As luck would have it, you were not with Robin when you died, but Robin was in the car with your spouse at the time of the accident, leaving Karl as the guardian of your children.

This was not the worst-case scenario, but it was not ideal either. Karl and Robin married only a year before your death. Though you liked him, you did not know him well enough to entrust him with your children. And your children barely know Karl at all.

Karl is a good, responsible man. He cherishes his wife's memory, and as an extension of her, he loves all of her friends. He wants to respect your wishes, so he agrees to serve as guardian of your children. After all, he has no evidence that you wanted otherwise, and he assumes that his religious affiliation guided your choice.

If you had worked with a Personal Family Lawyer, you would have named Robin and Karl as your first choice, but only if the couple remained married. You would have built in a provision to indicate that if the Couches divorced or if either of them died, your children would be raised by Patsy and Gus Garcia.

When your spouse dies, your children are in the care of the Garcias, who locate the guardianship paperwork you have given them and call the police.

Karl is consumed with grief over Robin's death, but he feels a moral obligation to follow your apparent wishes to assume permanent guardianship, and he begins the guardianship process.

In the meantime, your brother learns of your spouse's death.

Your brother earns a large salary as the area's leading oncologist. His wife, your sister-in-law, is a homemaker. She is a member of the

PTA. She is a charming socialite who serves on the boards of several nonprofits and volunteers her time for charities. The couple sends their children to the best school available. They live in a large home and seem to value education. They are picture-perfect.

Except, of course, for your sister-in-law's constant tirades. And let's not forgot your brother, who is a workaholic. Or their junior high school children, who have had their self-esteem trampled on for so many years that they have already started to turn to marijuana and alcohol to self-medicate.

Upon learning of your spouse's death, your brother and sister-in-law immediately challenge the guardianship. Karl feels relieved. He is a man who would never shirk his obligation to care for Carlos and Sara, but he is overwhelmed. Karl does not know anything about your brother, but he hopes that the courts grant him custody, and he withdraws his guardianship petition. He feels as if he's been let off the hook. *This is the perfect solution!* Karl thinks.

But when Gus and Patsy hear that your brother has challenged the guardianship, they file for guardianship. Gus and Patsy know all the sordid details about your brother and his wife.

The ensuing custody battle is long and drawn out, with your children right in the middle. Gus and Patsy, concerned with the well-being of your children, accuse your brother and sister-in-law of being terrible parents. Though Gus and Patsy's accusation is fair and necessary, you never would have wanted it made in a public forum. Embarrassed and hurt, your brother and sister-in-law dig up dirt on the Garcias.

What they find should be innocuous—in any other context, it would have been meaningless and harmless. But in this situation, it is detrimental. Your brother and sister-in-law find that Gus was arrested for indecent exposure while in college. Of course, you already knew this, because Gus moved into your neighborhood during college. In fact, you and your spouse were with him on the night in question, a night that involved too much beer and Gus's need to urinate right then and there—in public.

At the time, the event was embarrassing. In his adult years, it was fodder for jokes. One way or another, it was the innocent mistake of a young college student. Gus is an amazing father, a role model, and one of the best men you knew.

The courts don't know what to make of the situation. On the one hand, Gus and Patsy are high on your list of potential guardians. On the other hand, they are concerned with the best interests of your child, and your brother and sister-in-law appear picture-perfect.

What do the courts decide?

Turn to page 43.

You and Your Spouse Did Not Name Permanent Guardians.

You considered what would happen if both you and your spouse died at the same time. In fact, your parents were together when they died. Your father was an airline pilot who also had a private pilot's license. Though he was an expert pilot, the single-engine plane he was flying could not handle the unexpected storm while he and your mother were flying the short trip from Los Angeles to Santa Barbara.

The first time you and your spouse discussed naming a permanent guardian, you ended up in a fight. The second time, you ended up unable to choose between two couples.

Ultimately, you and your spouse wanted your children to be raised by people who lived in your neighborhood, who shared your spiritual values, and who had similar parenting philosophies. You considered which couples were well traveled, ones who valued foreign experiences and spoke several languages. This left only two couples: Patricia and Gus Garcia and Robin and Karl Couch.

Though the Couches are less affluent than the Garcias, they share your religious values and your parenting philosophy. The Garcias are the picture of culture. Their children know all about art and philosophy. They speak three languages and travel to South America for Christmas and France for summer vacations.

Both couples would have made excellent choices. You would have chosen Gus and Patsy. Your spouse was unsure but was leaning toward the Couches.

Secretly, you told the Garcias that you wanted them to be the guardians of your children. But you never documented anything. You considered making an appointment with a lawyer to help you reach a consensus, but you never got around to it.

You and your spouse did agree, in no uncertain terms, that you did not under any circumstance want your brother or sister-in-law to have custody of your children. Your sister-in-law is emotionally and verbally abusive to her own children. Your brother ignores the situation. Instead, he works sixteen-hour days, neglecting his family as it spirals out of control.

Had you made an appointment with a lawyer specifically trained to plan from a parent's perspective, you would have been advised to confidentially (but specifically) exclude your brother and sister-in-law from guardianship of your children in the event of your death or disability. The document would have specified that no matter what, your brother and sister-in-law would never be named guardian of your children under any situation. You would have created one, had you known.

It would have been a good idea.

As soon as your brother and sister-in-law learn of your spouse's death, they hire an attorney and petition the court for custody of Carlos and Sara. The Garcias, who know all of the sordid details about your brother and sister-in-law, also petition the court, requesting custody of your kids.

Your brother is the area's foremost oncologist, and your sister-in-law is a member of the PTA. She is charming and beautiful. She is married to a prominent doctor. She sends her children to the best private school available. She lives in a large house and values education.

On paper, the couple looks perfect. Your brother's large salary allows your sister-in-law to stay at home. The Garcias are a two-income family, and both work full-time jobs.

When your brother and sister-in-law challenge the petition for guardianship, the courts waste little time. The never meet the Garcias or your brother and sister-in-law. They simply look at the petitions and make a decision.

What do the courts decide?

Turn to page 43.

Your Brother and Sister-in-Law

The courts chose your brother and sister-in-law because they are family and look great on paper. They do not share your spiritual values, and they certainly do not share your parenting philosophy. They are close-minded and never encourage your children to grow and experience new things. They do not fit any of the criteria you had considered when considering guardians.

Your children move across the country with an uncle and aunt they do not know. They become influenced by their aunt. They rarely see their uncle and do not have the love and compassion they need.

Carlos becomes more and more withdrawn. He never laughs. Your brother and sister-in-law value academia but not the arts. They forbid Carlos to take art classes. Carlos struggles through school and is teased and bullied by the other children. In junior high school, Sara starts drinking; in high school, she starts experimenting with drugs. And both miss out on the little things: the countries and cultures you wanted your children to experience, the foreign language and music lessons that were so important to you.

In fact, your children grow into adults that behave nothing like you or your spouse. Sara behaves like your sister-in-law, Carlos like your brother.

Did you increase your family wealth or leave the world a better place? To choose a different outcome, return to page 1 and choose a different life and legacy for your children.

ADDITIONAL RESOURCES:
For Choosing the Right Guardians and Legally Documenting Your Choices

*T*he guardian of your children is the person responsible for taking care of your children's physical, emotional, and spiritual needs if you are unable to care for them. Approximately 69 percent of parents have not named legal guardians for their kids.[1] Of the 31 percent who have, most have made one of these common mistakes:

1. Naming a married couple to act as guardians and failing to provide instructions in case the named couple divorces or suffers the death of one spouse.

2. Not naming sufficient alternate guardians to serve if your first choice is unavailable.

3. Considering financial resources when deciding who should raise your children. Your guardians

---

[1] Cheryl Allebrand. "57% of Americans Do Not Have a Will." Bankrate, Inc., 19 Nov. 2007.
http://investor.bankrate.com/releasedetail.cfm?ReleaseID=276290.

do not have to also be financial decision makers for your kids. They should be the people who will make the best health care, education, housing, discipline, and care decisions for your kids. It is your responsibility to leave enough money behind to take care of your kids either through savings or life insurance; you can and should name someone other than the guardians of your children as guardians of the estate.

4. Not providing for someone to take care of the money you are leaving behind.

5. Naming only long-term care guardians and not making any arrangements for the immediate care of your children following your death or incapacity.

6. Not excluding anyone who might challenge your guardian decisions.

If you have minor children, regardless of the size of your bank account, you must legally document your decisions about who would raise your children if you cannot.

You can legally document your guardian choices for free at www. KidsProtectionPlan.com. You will also find a simple nine-step system for making sure that your children will never be taken out of your home or raised by anyone you would not want serving as guardian and that the money you leave behind will be well taken care of by the right people.

Upon completing all nine steps, you can rest assured that your children will be raised in accordance with your values, insights, stories, and experiences, growing into adults who would make you proud, are self-sufficient, and are satisfied with life.

What about the money, real estate, or other assets you will leave behind?

To make sure that the money you leave behind for your kids is immediately available to your kids' guardians and/or another person you trust to make financial decisions for your kids—without having to go through an unnecessary, expensive, time-consuming, and public court process and possibly incur estate taxes—turn to Story Two and Story Three, where you will learn to protect your assets.

STORY TWO:
Chelsea and Alex

You Leave Behind Millions, but How Will Your Child and Spouse Handle Life Without You?

Y ou know all about wills, or at least you think you do. When your grandmother died, she left you a bit of money, which meant that you were suddenly in need of a will of your own. You turned to Mr. Thomas, the family attorney who handled your grandparents' estate distribution and your parents' wills. Upon meeting with Mr. Thomas, you were impressed with his vast knowledge and ability to educate you. Mr. Thomas had been drafting Wills for forty-five years, and you trusted him totally.

That was seven years ago. You have since married Alex, and together you have worked hard to increase your savings. You and Alex own a small home in Santa Monica, a real estate hotbed adjacent to Los Angeles, and when you add everything, including your life insurance and the fair market value of your home, your children would receive an inheritance of almost three million dollars if you died.

Calculating the Value of Your Taxable Estate:

* Equity in real property—This is the amount left after paying your mortgage and any other debts associated with your property.

* Bank accounts

* Brokerage accounts—This includes your savings, investment, and checking accounts.

* Value of business interests—Any business you own, or any percentage of a business owned by you, is included in the value of your estate.

* Retirement accounts

* Death benefit from insurance policies

This reflects the size of your estate that is subject to estate tax. If your 2008 estate exceeds $2 million, your estate could be subject to a 45 percent estate tax! Estate tax is federal, which means you are subject to it regardless of where you live.

The total value of your taxable estate is a bit different than the total value of your probate estate. Probate is state specific. To calculate your total probate estate, visit www.FamilyWealth-Matters.com for a state-specific probate calculator.

You and Alex are planners. You plan to start a family in two years once your careers are established, figuring you can both afford to take time away from work once you have a little more experience. Before your children are even conceived, you establish a $40,000 college savings plan for the children you know you will have with the money your grandmother left. Of course, each of you has a life insurance plan.

When baby Chelsea arrives, you feel the urgent need to update your will, which was drafted seven years ago before you were married and before Chelsea was born. You need to make sure that you and Alex have wills that address your future as a couple, especially now that you have a child.

You want to schedule an appointment with Mr. Thomas, a seasoned veteran who has been loyal and trustworthy. Alex has read about lawyers who are specifically trained to plan for the needs of parents with young children, and Alex really wants to meet with a Personal Family Lawyer instead.

You suggest a compromise: "Let's make an appointment with both Mr. Thomas and a Personal Family Lawyer. We can make up our minds after we meet with both of them."

Mr. Thomas is near retirement and has a light client load, so he schedules your visit immediately. He is pleased to see you. You explain your situation, and Mr. Thomas agrees that you should update your will and that Alex should also have a will. He barely asks any questions before telling you that he can send Alex's will and an updated copy of your will the following week. He suggests that you leave everything to each other and then, upon the second spouse's death, to Chelsea.

Alex is skeptical. "He didn't ask any questions," Alex says. Still, Alex is impressed with the sense of urgency Mr. Thomas displays.

"Of course he didn't ask a lot of questions," you say. "He's been drafting wills for over fifty years. He could do this in his sleep."

Alex is convinced. "Let's cancel our meeting with the other lawyer," Alex says on the way home. "It all seems very boilerplate. If I die, everything will go to you. If you die, everything will go to me. If we both die, it all goes to Chelsea, obviously. We don't need to visit another attorney to tell us that."

If you agree with Alex and decide to hire Mr. Thomas without meeting the other attorney, turn to page 53. Otherwise, turn to page 55.

You Decide to Plan with Mr. Thomas.

You and Alex agree that Mr. Thomas's more than fifty years of experience trumps anything the Personal Family Lawyer might have said, and you call Mr. Thomas immediately to tell him your decision. Mr. Thomas says that he will mail your wills the following week.

Your wills arrive on schedule. The documents look standard. If you die, everything goes to Alex. If Alex dies, everything goes to you. If you both die, everything goes to Chelsea. Alex's sister, Kaari, who lives in the same city, is named as Chelsea's guardian. In case Kaari is unable to assume guardianship, Alex's parents are your backup choice. You name your parents as executors of your will and guardians of the estate; if they die, Kaari is the backup choice.

Speaking of your new daughter, Chelsea is a handful! As a result, you and Alex both take eight-week leaves of absence from work to care for Chelsea. Unfortunately, when you return to work, your company immediately sends you on an emergency out-of-town trip. You are heartbroken to leave Chelsea and Alex, and your company promises not to send you on any more trips for at least six months.

You are sent to a small, quaint town in Northern California. Because this is a last-minute trip, you are unable to find a hotel room and instead are one of three guests in the local bed and breakfast.

The same day you arrive, a contractor running an electricity conduit under a road unknowingly pierces a propane line. Unbeknownst to anyone, the propane has settled directly underneath the bed and breakfast. While you are sleeping, the propane explodes, killing you, the owners of the bed and breakfast, and two other guests.

With a two-month-old baby to care for, Alex has no time to grieve. Your assets, which you and Alex held jointly, are transferred to Alex directly, with no estate tax and no court involvement. The one million dollars of life insurance is deposited into Alex's bank account.

Does Alex remarry? If so, turn to page 67. If not, turn to page 71.

You Keep Your Appointment with the Personal Family Lawyer.

Despite your comfort level with Mr. Thomas, Alex's initial resistance has transferred to you. "There is no harm is seeking a second opinion," you tell Alex.

Together, you and Alex find a Personal Family Lawyer by visiting www.PersonalFamilyLawyer.com. Natalie ("Nat") Henson's office is just moments from your home. When you call to make an appointment with Nat, you can already tell that the visit with Nat is going to be an entirely different experience. Nat's scheduling assistant explains that Nat only takes on a few new clients a month because her focus is on creating a lifetime relationship that is personal to each client family. You have to wait several weeks for an appointment, but Nat's assistant assures you that she will send a premeeting package so that you can begin to prepare for the meeting.

The preparation package you receive before the meeting asks all sorts of questions about your family, your values, and your assets. As you complete the worksheets, you are surprised to find out just how much you have to pass along. You start thinking about answers to questions like these:

- ❖ Who would raise Chelsea if you could not? Are your parents really the best choice, or should you consider close friends who share your parenting values?

- ❖ Who will guard the money that you leave behind for Chelsea?

- ❖ Do you want Chelsea to receive her inheritance outright, or would you prefer that she receive it at an age-appropriate time designated by you? Or, even better, in a lifetime protected trust that she can control when she is old enough but will be safe from a future divorce or lawsuits?

❖ If you die first, do you want Alex to have the ability to leave the money you have acquired together to a future spouse?

You had no idea there was so much to think about. Mr. Thomas did not mention any of this during your brief meeting.

When you arrive for your appointment, Nat greets you with a smile. Nat is quite a bit younger than Mr. Thomas, and she begins by telling you how the law firm works and what makes her practice different from the traditional and, in her opinion, antiquated practice of estate planning.

Nat describes the typical estate planning experience. It sounds just like the experience you had with Mr. Thomas!

Nat explains that in the traditional experience, clients meet with a lawyer who prepares form documents, which the clients sign without really understanding all of their options completely. The clients then take those documents home, mark "Estate Planning" off their checklists, put the documents in a drawer or on a shelf, and never look at them again.

"The unfortunate part," Nat says, "is that the planning documents are stale almost as soon as the clients leave the office. On top of the fact that the client never really understood the documents, their lives change, their assets change, and even the law changes, but those documents just stay the same."

And even though people know that things have changed, they are reluctant to call their lawyers, because they know they will be billed hourly in six-minute increments for each call. Nat tells you that she billed four hundred dollars per hour when she worked at a big, traditional law firm!

Nat then goes on to explain that when clients called her old law firm, she was often unable to respond to even quick questions for hours or days at a time, because she did not have a support team; she was the only person responsible for taking care of all the planning details.

As a result, she saw a lot of plans fail when families needed it the most and when it was too late: after death or incapacity. Assets were owned incorrectly, documents were outdated, and family members did not know what to do or where to turn during an already emotionally difficult time.

Nat says that she went to law school to make a difference in people's lives, to be a lifetime advisor, and then to be there for a client's family when the client cannot be. Until she became a Personal Family Lawyer, Nat was seriously disappointed with her career choice.

Nat explains that working with a Personal Family Lawyer is a totally different experience. First of all, Personal Family Lawyers do not charge hourly fees, which means you can call anytime without receiving a bill in the mail a couple of weeks later.

She talks about her team, which is available during office hours to answer quick questions and around the clock to address emergencies. If you need to talk with her about something more strategic or legal in nature, Nat assures you that she will be available for a scheduled call, so you will never have to leave dozens of messages back and forth.

Then Nat tells you that your plan is certain to work over time, because she will review it at least every three years for no additional charge. She also tells you about a membership program that will allow you to update your planning and get ongoing legal guidance for life without paying hourly fees!

Best of all, Nat talks about helping you pass on more than just your financial wealth to Chelsea. She introduces the concept of "whole family wealth," explaining that financial wealth is just a small part of a person's wealth. The most important parts of family wealth are actually intangible assets such as intellectual, spiritual, and human assets or values, insights, stories, and experience.

Nat tells you that these intangible assets are most often lost when someone dies. "Think about your own grandparents or great-grandparents," Nat says. "What do you know about them?"

You realize that you know very little about your parents' grandparents. Indeed, you do not even know their first names. Your grandmother left you a nice financial inheritance, but none of her childhood stories or experiences were captured. She might have passed on her values to you, but how much of these values will you consciously pass on to your children in honor of your grandparents? It dawns on you that Chelsea will never hear your grandma's voice telling her how much she loves her. And it bothers you that if the tradition continues, Chelsea's grandchildren will not even know your name.

Nat says she uses a tool called a Family Wealth Legacy Interview, which is designed to capture and pass on these intangible assets. It all feels so much more personalized, which comforts you as you consider Chelsea's future.

Nat explains that the first step is to discuss exactly what would happen to Chelsea and your money as things currently stand. If you are unhappy with the status quo, Nat tells you she can help create a plan to make sure that your daughter, your assets, your values, and your legacy are protected in the event of your death or incapacity.

You are shocked when Nat tells you what would happen if you left your future in the hands of a will.

It turns out that because your parents and Alex's parents all live across the United States, Chelsea could actually be taken into foster care temporarily if anything happens to you and Alex!

Mr. Thomas did not mention anything about this.

As you discuss the scenario with Nat, you can see how obvious it is. If anything happened to you, your wills would be at Mr. Thomas's office, and no one would even know where to find them. Your parents would be hours away, and the authorities would not have any instructions on how you want Chelsea cared for in the meantime.

Of course, the police would call in Child Protective Services, and they would have no choice but to take Chelsea from your home. You are shocked that Mr. Thomas failed to tell you this critical information!

You are even more shocked when Nat shows you how ill protected your money is with just wills.

First of all, your house and bank accounts, as well as most of your holdings (except life insurance and certain retirement accounts), would have to go through a long and expensive court process called probate. This means that the money you left behind would be tied up in court for twelve to eighteen months, minimum.[2] And the court process could cost your family as much as $150,000,[3] with much of that going to Mr. Thomas!

---

[2] Per the California probate system. States each have their own probate processes, some of which are more onerous than others. Consult a Personal Family Lawyer in your state for specifics about what will happen if your assets go through probate.

[3] In California, the cost of probate is approximately 5 percent of the gross estate (meaning fair market value). To calculate the cost of probate for your family, contact a lawyer in your state.

You are blown away to discover that when both you and Alex die, you will have to pay estate taxes. You and Alex do not feel like rich people, but because of your life insurance and home, you have nearly three million dollars in assets, which means you are subject to the estate tax.[4]

If you die and Alex lives, the wills offer no protection at all against future spouses, which means that Alex can remarry and give all of your assets to a new spouse. And worst of all, if both you and Alex die, Chelsea could inherit everything outright and totally unprotected when she turns eighteen.

Nat asks you and Alex to each share the one thing you wish you could change about the current plan.

It is hard for you to know where to start.

You and Alex agree that guardianship issues are your highest concerns. With respect to finances, you are most concerned with the probate process. Though you are not particularly concerned about the cost of probate, you do not want to put your family through twelve to eighteen months of court and lawyers. You want to make it as easy as possible for them if anything happens to you.

Alex, on the other hand, is particularly concerned about the estate taxes. At 45 percent, the tax would mean that $450,000 of your $1-million life insurance policy would go straight to the government.

"The good news," says Nat, "is that we can make sure there is no court process at all and no estate taxes. Both of those things are voluntary. The only people who have to deal with probate and

---

[4] As of 2008, any estate in excess of two million dollars is subject to the federal estate tax.

estate taxes are family members of people who do not plan or who plan improperly.

According to federal tax law, the first $2 million of an estate (in 2008) is not subject to the estate tax. We call this amount the "exempt" amount because it is exempt from estate tax (it is not taxed). This exemption is given to each person. As such, you might think that a married couple has $4 million worth of exemptions, right? Unfortunately, in many cases, because of the way assets are owned by the married couple, this is not right; if you are like 69 percent of married couples, who have never worked with a lawyer to ensure assets are owned in the right way so as to take advantage of each exemption, you will lose one of the $2 million exemptions upon death and all assets in excess of $2 million will be subject to estate tax at a rate of 45 percent. On a $3 million estate, your family would lose $450,000 to estate taxes!

"All we have to do is take your house and bank accounts and put them into a revocable living trust. Then we name the trust as the beneficiary of your life insurance policies and as the second beneficiary on your retirement accounts. Your spouse will remain the first beneficiary.

"Once we do that," Nat tells you, "your assets will not go through probate. Chelsea or her guardian could *immediately* access them per the terms you specify."

Nat turns to Alex. "And the assets would be free of any and all estate taxes so long as your assets stay below four million dollars. We can even protect Chelsea's inheritance so that it is never at risk if she gets divorced or if a lawsuit is filed against her when she is an adult."

According to federal tax codes, the first $2 million of an estate are not subject to the estate tax. We call this the "$2 million estate tax coupon." This coupon applies to an estate, not an individual. In other words, a married couple is given only one $2 million coupon, unless the couple establishes a Trust or otherwise structures the ownership of their assets to use both coupons, in which case $4 million is exempt from estate taxes.

"That sounds great," says Alex. "But I'm not entirely sure I know what a trust is."

Nat explains that a trust is an agreement between the person who has assets to put into the trust (also called the grantor, trustor, trust-maker, or settlor) and the trustee, who agrees to hold those assets for the benefit of the beneficiary.

"There are three important roles in a trust agreement: the *grantor*, who gives assets to the *trustee*, who holds them for the benefit of the *beneficiary*. The trust agreement is basically just a set of instructions telling the trustee how you want everything handled.

"While you are both living, you are in all three of those important roles. You are the grantor, the trustee, and the beneficiary, so you have not given anything up by putting your assets into the trust.

"Think of a trust as a treasure chest in which you store all your assets, including your home, your investments, your savings accounts, and everything else you own," Nat continues. "Once you put your assets in the treasure chest, you do not own them—your treasure chest does. But you can open that treasure chest anytime you want. You have full control of everything in the treasure chest."

"This sounds too good to be true," you say. "Are there any downsides?"

"Here's the amazing part," says Nat. "There is no downside to having your assets in a trust. Sure, it will cost you some money—approximately three to six thousand dollars[5]—to get it set up, but the

---

[5] This approximation varies by lawyer and by state. Be wary of attorneys whose fees are significantly less than this, as a sharply reduced rate would likely indicate that you are merely buying documents instead of hiring a lawyer who focuses on guiding you through a lifetime of the right decisions and who will be there for your family when you cannot be. In that case, your estate plan is likely to fail when your family most needs it.

cost is far less than the cost of probate, estate taxes, and the night-mare not having a trust will create for your family. Plus it will start a lifetime relationship with our law firm, so you will have somewhere to turn throughout your life. And the best part is that we will be here for your family when you cannot be.

"And if you move to another state or something happens to me, you do not have to worry because we have a Personal Family Lawyer in every neighborhood.

"The most important thing you need to know when establishing a trust is that you need to make sure that all of your assets are owned correctly in the name of the trust, always. If you are working with our firm, you do not have to worry too much about it now. We will guide you through the whole process. And we will make sure that your plan continues to work throughout your lifetime, by reviewing it regularly. No doubt your life, your assets, and the law will change many, many times before your death, and we will want to maintain your trust accordingly.

"If all that sounds good, we can go through a series of questions that will allow me to design the best possible plan for you and your family."

You and Alex do not even need to discuss it; the choice is obvi-ous. "I'm sold," you say to Alex, who nods enthusiastically in agree-ment. "This is our Personal Family Lawyer."

You turn back to Nat and say, "Let's get started."

Over the next forty-five minutes, you answer questions you never had thought about. When you leave, you feel a tremendous peace and calm, knowing that everything will be taken care of if anything hap-pens to you.

You call Mr. Thomas and tell him that you have decided to go with another attorney. You feel slightly guilty, so you thank him for all the work he has done for your family and ask if you can take him to lunch.

Over lunch, you explain your decision. Mr. Thomas understands and admits that he is less familiar with trusts than he ought to be. He is retiring the following month and calls himself an "old-fashioned attorney." You feel less guilty when Mr. Thomas says, "You sound like you are in good hands. I won't have to worry about you when I retire." Mr. Thomas asks to see a picture of Chelsea, who is almost five weeks old.

"She is a delight, but Alex and I have our hands full!" you say.

In the coming weeks, your new attorney establishes your trust and guides you and Alex through the transfer of your assets into the trust, all while you and Alex are out on parenting leave.

Unfortunately, as soon as your leave ends, your company immediately sends you on an emergency out-of-town trip. You are heartbroken to leave Chelsea and Alex so soon, and your company promises not to send you on any more trips for at least six months.

You are sent to a small, quaint town in Northern California. Because this is a last-minute trip, you are unable to find a hotel room. Instead, you are one of three guests in the local bed and breakfast.

The same day you arrive, a contractor running an electricity conduit under a road unknowingly pierces a propane line. Unbeknownst to anyone, the propane has settled directly underneath the bed and breakfast. While you are sleeping, the propane explodes, killing you, the owners of the bed and breakfast, and two other guests.

With a two-month-old baby to care for, Alex has little time to grieve. Alex calls Nat, and together they move the assets as directed by the trust. Your $1-million life insurance policy is put into a special trust that Alex controls and can use but that Alex cannot give away to anyone other than Chelsea. The trust also provides that its assets cannot be taken from Alex in the event of a lawsuit. Pursuant to Nat's advice, Alex puts half of the assets you acquired together during your marriage into this second, protected trust as well.

Does Alex remarry? If so, turn to page 79. If not, turn to page 87.

Alex Remarries with the Wills Provided by Mr. Thomas

Heartbroken, Alex spends several years trying to move forward and finds comfort only in work and your daughter, Chelsea. Alex works day and night, turning the three million dollars into four million. Doctors and friends tell Alex to slow down, but work helps ease the pain of your death.

Luckily, Alex meets JJ, a co-worker and another work-first go-getter. JJ has sole custody of two children from a former marriage as well as a mountain of debt from the first marriage. Eventually JJ and Alex marry and do what most couples do: combine their assets. They have joint bank accounts, their home is owned in both JJ and Alex's names, credit card accounts are held jointly, and Alex pays off JJ's debts.

Although both JJ and Alex work too much, Chelsea and her two stepsiblings are relatively happy and well-adjusted children. Alex and JJ are both good providers who want the best for all three children. They are so focused on their careers, though, that they are somewhat neglectful and indifferent when it comes to providing emotional support and involvement. But the three stepsiblings are close. And because Alex and JJ are so well off, the children are able to participate in many school activities and find support in extended networks of school friends, parents, coaches, teachers, and the like.

In what seems like the blink of an eye, sixteen years pass from the time of your death.

And then, at the young age of fifty, Alex dies. For those who knew Alex, this was not a big surprise. Alex was bound to have a heart attack, given the stress and fatigue associated with working sixteen-hour days. In fact, since your death sixteen years prior, Alex had not taken more than a few days of vacation. Upon Alex's death, Alex's $4-million estate (which includes the assets you left when you died) goes directly to JJ, as Alex's surviving spouse. Nothing goes to Chelsea.

Chelsea suffers tremendously over the loss of Alex. Luckily, she has loving stepsiblings and a staunch support network through school and all of her extracurricular activities. She is also lucky because JJ thinks of Chelsea as her own child and does not think twice about supporting Chelsea in the same way Alex would have.

When Chelsea graduates from high school, she is able to attend the university of her choosing. She scored high grades throughout high school and had numerous sporting and other extracurricular activities on her résumé. Between the grants and scholarships she received and JJ's assets (primarily the assets you and Alex earned that Alex grew), no limits are set on the money Chelsea can spend pursuing higher education. She excels in the sciences, intends to attend graduate school, and ultimately wants a job in the field of biotechnology. Through your hard work, and that of Alex and JJ, Chelsea has everything going for her.

But then, during Chelsea's sophomore year, JJ dies while driving home late from cocktails with an important client.

Although unfailingly committed to Chelsea in life, Alex and JJ had not made plans to ensure an equitable distribution of assets upon their death.

JJ's will was signed before even meeting Alex. JJ had always meant to get around to updating it but never did. At JJ's death, the estate goes through a long, expensive probate and is subject to estate tax of 45 percent for each dollar over two million. Because nothing was ever put in trust after Alex's death, neither Chelsea nor her stepsiblings have access to the funds during the probate process.

When all is said and done, the $4 million estate left by Alex is worth $2.9 million. The probate process cost $200,000, and the rest was absorbed by estate taxes.

Not that Chelsea receives a single penny. Because JJ was the last to die, JJ's children inherit the entirety of the remaining estate. Chelsea no longer has access to any of the money that was being used to pay for her education, her housing, her books, her personal items, or her health insurance. Chelsea will have to figure out how to pay her tuition for next semester, not to mention the cost of attending graduate school.

Chelsea will have to rely on the generosity of her stepsiblings, who, though they love Chelsea, are not too keen on sharing their inheritance.

Your choices created a situation in which your daughter receives no inheritance. Instead, everything you worked so hard for before your death is distributed to people you did not even know, including one million dollars paid to the government. To choose a different legacy, go back to page 49 and make different choices.

Alex Does Not Remarry with the Wills Provided by Mr. Thomas

Heartbroken, Alex spends years trying to move forward and finds comfort only in work and your daughter, Chelsea. Alex, who works day and night, turns the $3-million estate you left behind into $4 million. Doctors say Alex should slow down, but work helps ease the pain of your death.

Alex never considers updating the will you executed together. After all, it clearly specifies that your assets will be transferred to Chelsea upon both of her parents' deaths. This is exactly what Alex wants, so there seems to be no need to revisit Mr. Thomas. After your death, Mr. Thomas never said anything different.

Despite the tragedy of your death, Chelsea is a happy child, and she grows into a happy teenager. She does wish that Alex would spend less time at work and more time with her, but rather than complain, she copes by emulating Alex's workaholic mentality and earns high grades at school.

And then sixteen years later, Alex dies. For those who knew Alex, this was not a big surprise. Alex was bound to have a heart attack, given the stress and fatigue associated with working sixteen-hour days. In fact, since your death, Alex had not taken more than a few days of vacation.

Chelsea immediately shuts down upon Alex's death. Your sister-in-law, Kaari, whom you and Alex named as guardian in your will, assumes custody of Chelsea. Kaari is a nurse who works evenings, which means that Chelsea is often alone at night, and she feels lonely, devastated, and abandoned. Though your sister-in-law is committed to your daughter's happiness, she simply is not home enough to comfort Chelsea.

Kaari considers finding a different job, but the economy is unkind, and though she submits hundreds of résumés, her search is unsuccessful.

The only other option she can imagine is quitting her job to become a full-time parent, but she is disheartened to hear that your assets are going through the long and arduous probate court process.

Mr. Thomas's son, Kent Thomas, Jr., has taken over the wills Mr. Thomas prepared for you. He explains to Kaari that Alex's assets will be tied up in court for at least one year and possibly as long as eighteen months. He explains that probate is basically a lawsuit filed against Alex's estate for the benefit of Alex's creditors. It is a system that the courts use to protect potential creditors of your estate and to order the distribution of your estate.

Normally, Alex's life insurance would have paid right away, but because Chelsea is not yet an adult and the life insurance was designated to her as the beneficiary, the court will have to designate a financial guardian for Chelsea before the life insurance can be distributed. Kent Thomas, Jr. explains that the process could cost the $4-million estate approximately 5 percent (or $200,000). Worst of all, because of Kaari's poor credit, she cannot get bonded and will not be able to be the financial guardian. You and Alex named your parents as the financial guardians when you first created your wills so many years before, but your parents died five years earlier. The court will have to appoint an expensive professional guardian at $125 an hour.

Kaari struggles through the next year. She discovers that Chelsea has not been coming home at night. Furthermore, Kaari suspects that she has started drinking. Chelsea is no longer an honor student. She is obviously having problems.

Kaari is overjoyed when she learns that the probate court has finally finished with Alex's estate; however, she is shocked to learn that in addition to probate fees, the estate also paid nearly a million dollars in taxes! All of your assets were in Alex's name, so Alex's estate totaled four million dollars at the time of death. Because assets over two million dollars are subject to estate taxes, two million dollars were subject to a 45 percent estate tax, or nine hundred thousand dollars.

Chelsea is three months away from turning eighteen.

During these three months, Chelsea and Kaari continue to fight nonstop. Kaari wants Chelsea to stay living with her, to continue with therapy, but Chelsea refuses. She will soon be a millionaire, and she wants to live alone.

When she turns eighteen, Chelsea moves into an apartment of her own. Angry with Kaari, Chelsea cuts off all contact. Kaari has spent the last twenty-two months taking an emotional and financial beating while trying to care for Chelsea. Now Kaari feels broken. She has no energy left to fight with Chelsea, reason with her, or save her from the destructive will of an eighteen-year-old with a seemingly endless stream of money. Kaari gives up and tries to put some remnant of a life back together for herself.

Left to her own devices, and with what an eighteen-year-old would consider a large fortune, Chelsea rents a nice apartment and does not bother to apply to any universities.

Instead, with high school finished and no reason to get a job, she spends more and more time with her friends. Although they are not terrible people, they are not the caliber of people Chelsea would be spending time with had she attended a university. Not surprisingly, with too much time on her hands, not enough structure in her life, and having lost both of her parents young, Chelsea soon marries a man about a decade older than she is.

In a way, her husband is good for her. He is a little showy, drives expensive cars, buys fancy suits, and flashes money to impress people, but Nick is not a bad man. Nick is a clinical researcher in the bio-tech industry, which had always interested Chelsea. He provides some structure and maturity in her life, and Chelsea shifts her focus from partying to helping Nick in his business endeavors. She stops staying out late and begins to concentrate her energy on her home life and helping her husband.

Chelsea is not particularly educated or mature when it comes to finances, and she and Nick simply combine all of their assets, as most couples do. Chelsea assumes, from Nick's behavior, that he has an ample amount of assets, and she leaves the family bookkeeping to him.

Like many marriages, Chelsea and Nick's relationship has its ups and downs. Within a few years of the marriage, Chelsea starts questioning her relationship with Nick.

Does she seek a divorce? If so, turn to page 75. If not, turn to page 77.

Chelsea and Nick Divorce

As Chelsea ages, she also begins to mature. Though she loves Nick, she wonders if she was too young to marry. She wants to attend college and pursue a career of her own. Nick, on the other hand, is not interested in having anything other than a stand-by-her-man wife. He wants to be with someone who will raise his children and support his career. Though Chelsea wants to do both of those things, she also wants to pursue her own independence.

After what seems like an endless stream of fights, Chelsea and Nick decide to divorce amicably. But the situation quickly turns ugly when Chelsea realizes that Nick had few assets when he and Chelsea married. Instead, Nick spent a sizeable chunk of Chelsea's inheritance. Because the couple combined assets when they married, he now owns half of the inheritance that you worked so hard to leave Chelsea.

If this is not the life you wanted for Chelsea, return to page 49 and choose a different legacy.

Chelsea and Nick Remain Married

As Chelsea ages, she also begins to mature. Though she loves Nick, she realizes that she married far too young. She wants to attend college and pursue a career of her own. Nick, on the other hand, is not interested in having anything other than a stand-by-her-man wife. He wants to be with someone who will raise his children and support his career. Though Chelsea wants to do both of those things, she also wants to pursue her own independence.

After what seems like an endless stream of fights, Chelsea and Nick decide to seek counseling. Both are committed to making the marriage work, and as they progress and grow, they evolve into more mature, responsible adults who respect each other, growing a stronger relationship along the way.

Unfortunately, within several years of their marriage, Chelsea's husband is sued. Unbeknownst to him, one of Nick's biotech businesses had not obtained proper consent before harvesting tissue from donors. Because they have combined all of their assets, most of Chelsea's inheritance is lost, satisfying several judgments against her husband.

Chelsea does her best to remain supportive throughout her husband's legal troubles. But the lawsuits have nearly driven the couple into bankruptcy, and Chelsea is forced to take a job rather than attend college. She is angry and bitter, and she and Nick's marriage begins to deteriorate.

Is this the life you wanted for your daughter? If not, go back to page 49 and choose a different legacy.

Alex Remarries with a Trust

Heartbroken, Alex spends several years trying to move forward and finds comfort only in work and your daughter, Chelsea. Alex works day and night, turning the three million dollars you and Alex owned at the time of your death into four million. Doctors say Alex should slow down, but work helps ease the pain of your death.

Luckily, Alex meets JJ, a co-worker and another work-first go-getter. JJ has sole custody of two children from a former marriage. Eventually JJ and Alex marry. Because they work so hard, they might not have made time to think about planning, as most people do not. But the trust that you and Alex established together requires Alex to have a prenuptial agreement with any new spouse or be cut off from access to the special protected trust created after your death.

Before marrying JJ, Alex calls Nat, your Personal Family Lawyer, who prepares a prenuptial agreement for Alex and JJ to sign.[6] Nat prepares a trust for JJ and Alex's joint assets and a separate trust for the assets that JJ brings into their marriage. Nat reminds Alex how to maintain the separate assets acquired during your marriage. Nat assures Alex that if anything happens to Alex, your assets will go to Chelsea, not to JJ or JJ's children.

Although both JJ and Alex work too much, Chelsea and her two stepsiblings are relatively happy and well-adjusted children. Alex and JJ are both good providers who want the best for all three children. They are so focused on their careers that they are somewhat neglect-

---

[6] JJ must have separate counsel to sign off on the prenuptial agreement. In California, as in as many other states, a prenuptial agreement is only valid if each of the parties is represented by independent counsel. Contact a Personal Family Lawyer in your state for more guidance.

ful and indifferent when it comes to providing emotional support and involvement, but the three stepsiblings are close. And because Alex and JJ are so well off, the children are able to participate in many school activities and find support in extended networks of school friends, parents, coaches, teachers, and the like.

Then, sixteen years after your death, Alex dies. For those who knew Alex, this was not a big surprise. Alex was bound to have health issues, given the stress and fatigue associated with working sixteen-hour days. In fact, since your death, Alex had not taken more than a few days of vacation.

Chelsea suffers tremendously over the loss of Alex. Luckily, she has loving stepsiblings and a staunch support network through school and all of her extracurricular activities. She is also lucky to have JJ, who is committed, though benignly neglectful. Nevertheless, Chelsea cannot help but suffer from having lost both parents to untimely deaths. Moreover, despite all of their love and commitment, Chelsea cannot help but feel just a tiny bit like an outsider in her family, now that both biological parents are gone. She longs for people whose faces look like her own and who remember the inside jokes and little songs of her childhood.

Fortunately, ample money has been set aside in a trust specifically designated for Chelsea, and Nat is providing the trustee, your sister-in-law, Kaari, with guidance about how to use the money for Chelsea's benefit. Chelsea is able to receive grief counseling, and JJ is able to receive payments for the care of Chelsea. There is no need for a probate, and no estate taxes are paid.

The money in the trust is administered and supervised by Kaari, who was designated by you and Alex to act as trustee so long as she was not Chelsea's guardian

> *Wherever possible, it is a good idea to name two separate people as guardian (responsible for your children's physical, emotional, and spiritual wellbeing) and Trustee (responsible for your estate's financial wellbeing). This keeps checks-and-balances in place whereby the Trustee and guardian watch over each other to ensure that they are both acting in the best interest of your children.*

Kaari, Alex's sister, simply ensures that the money is used for its intended purpose: to care for Chelsea. JJ does not need to petition the court for access to the money. Instead, JJ and Kaari have worked out a regular schedule of trust distributions. JJ, as Chelsea's care guardian, makes requests to Kaari for extraordinary expenses, and Kaari promptly provides JJ with funds.

When Chelsea turns eighteen, she will be able to obtain funds directly from the trust with Kaari's approval. When she turns thirty, the trust that you and Alex created dictates that Chelsea will be old enough to control trust monies on her own.

The more guidance you can provide your chosen Trustee ("financial parent") about how you want Trust assets to be distributed to your child and/or their guardian, the better.

For most parents, this is hard to do: How do you even know where to start?

I am going to make it easy for you.

Visit www.FamilyWealthMatters.com and download your free Trustee Distribution Guidelines worksheet. In this worksheet, I walk you through 10 different types of life events you may want to consider supporting for your child, such as travel, career choices, weddings, business, and transportation. Plus, I give you three possible guidelines you can give a Trustee; select one of the examples I provide or use the samples to spark ideas to create your own.

Because you have structured the trust this way, Kaari is able to act as Chelsea's "financial parent" until Chelsea is mature enough to make her own financial decisions.

When Chelsea graduates from high school, she is able to attend the university of her choice. She scored high grades in high school and had numerous sporting and other extracurricular activities on her résumé. Between the grants and scholarships she received and the trust you and Alex set up for her, no limits are on the money she can spend pursuing higher education. She excels in the sciences, intends to attend graduate school, and ultimately wants a job in the field of biotechnology. Through the hard work of you and Alex, Chelsea has everything going for her.

Nevertheless, perhaps because she lost both of her parents so young, Chelsea ends up marrying young, and to an older man, a clinical researcher she met in one of the university's labs. Nick is a little showy, drives expensive cars, buys fancy suits, and flashes money to impress people. But he and Chelsea have similar interests, and Nick is a caring husband. He provides some structure and maturity in her life. Chelsea helps Nick in his business endeavors, and Nick helps Chelsea in her studies.

Because money is not an issue for Chelsea, she fails to discuss finances with Nick. But after graduating from college, Chelsea realizes several things about Nick. First of all, he has a mountain of debt and is up to his neck in credit card bills. He also lacks integrity in his business dealings. Unfortunately, within a few months of their marriage, Nick is sued because one of his biotech businesses was harvesting tissues without proper donor forms. Nick's own assets are decimated by the judgment, but because Chelsea's assets belong to the trust you set up for her, they are untouchable.

This experience, coupled with wisdom that comes with age, causes Chelsea to begin questioning her marriage to Nick. Chelsea wants to pursue a career of her own, Nick is not interested in having anything other than a stand-by-her-man wife. He wants to be with someone who will raise his children and support his career. Though Chelsea wants to do both of those things, she also wants to pursue her own independence.

Though she loves Nick, Chelsea wonders if she was rash in marrying Nick. After what seems like an endless stream of fights, Chelsea and Nick decide to divorce amicably. But the situation takes a twist when Nick tries to claim half of Chelsea's inheritance.

Chelsea's lawyer laughs when she hears the news. "Not a chance," Nat tells Nick. Nick's lawyer informs his client of the same. The money is protected by the trust you set up for Chelsea when she was just a little baby. Nick cannot touch it. Because her assets are held in trust, they cannot be reached by the divorce proceedings, and none of the money will be distributed to Chelsea's ex-husband as part of any dissolution settlement.

Chelsea is relieved to hear the news. Ready for a fresh start, Chelsea can use the money to start a business or attend graduate school, whatever her choosing. While her marriage definitely provided a setback in her life, Chelsea has the resources, education, and support network to move on and pursue her own dreams.

Turn to page 85.

Chelsea Goes to Graduate School

Chelsea is an avid learner, and she pursues first a PhD in biomedical research, later obtaining her medical degree with a specialty in cardiology, an interest that likely stemmed from Alex's heart attack. After years and years of school, Chelsea is thrilled to start her own practice alongside another doctor, Dr. Corbin, with whom she completed her fellowship and developed a romantic relationship.

Chelsea has chosen a high-risk profession. Immediately after their marriage, she and Dr. Corbin sit down with an attorney to discuss the liability insurance they must carry, as well as the proper structure to protect their business and assets from risk. Chelsea's attorney is impressed with the nearly bulletproof trust that you and Alex established for Chelsea. The attorney explains its benefits: if either Chelsea or Dr. Corbin is sued, a likely occurrence in the medical profession, the judgment cannot reach Chelsea's assets. This means the money will be available for Chelsea and your grandchildren, who come a few years after Chelsea and Dr. Corbin marry. The lawyer explains that the assets are further protected from any future spouses (Chelsea already knows about this!) or stepchildren, keeping the money for its intended recipients: your children and grandchildren.

Fortunately, Chelsea and her husband have a healthy medical practice and are never sued. They also have a healthy marriage and have three children. Because of your wise planning, your grandchildren, and even their children, benefit from the trust's assets, which are forever protected from creditors, predators, lawsuits, and future spouses.

Chelsea often gathers her children around to listen to the CD you recorded many years before when you met with your Personal Family

Lawyer to plan for your life and your legacy. Chelsea and your grand-children hear you and Alex talk about the life lessons you hoped to pass on and the love you felt for Chelsea. Despite Chelsea's despair at losing you, she and her children feel infinite peace and inner knowledge that everything will work out as it is supposed to, and they feel the loving embrace of an energy greater than themselves.

Congratulations. Your choice to plan for your life and your legacy had the lasting impact of increasing your whole family wealth for generations to come. You have left the world a better place. Turn to page 93 for more information about creating a legacy for your family.

Alex Does Not Remarry with a Trust.

Heartbroken, Alex spends years trying to move forward and finds comfort only in work and your daughter, Chelsea. Alex, who works day and night, quickly turns the $3-million estate into $4 million. Doctors say Alex should slow down, but work helps ease the pain of your death.

Despite the tragedy of your death, Chelsea is a relatively happy and well-adjusted child. She wishes Alex was home more, but rather than let it get her down, she decides to emulate Alex, and she throws herself into schoolwork, sports, and other extracurricular activities. She excels at the sciences and someday wants to work in the biotech field.

But Chelsea's stability is shattered when Alex dies. For those who knew Alex, it was not a big surprise. Alex was bound to have a heart attack, given the stress and fatigue associated with working sixteen-hour days. In fact, since your death sixteen years prior, Alex had not taken more than a few days of vacation.

Chelsea immediately shuts down upon Alex's death. Your sister-in-law, Kaari, whom you and Alex named as guardian in your will, assumes custody of Chelsea. Kaari is a nurse who works evenings; however, it takes no time at all for her to realize that Chelsea cannot be left home alone at night. At first, it does not seem feasible for Kaari to quit working in order to become a full-time parent—though that may be what Chelsea needs right now—and she worries about finding a daytime job in the slow economy.

Thank goodness you and Alex learned about trusts from Nat, your Personal Family Lawyer. Almost immediately after Alex's death,

Kaari calls Nat and learns that she can get nearly immediate access to all of the money in the trust to meet any of Chelsea's needs, including grief counseling, through the trustee you and Alex appointed to act as Chelsea's "financial parent."

> *Think of the Trustee as your child's "financial parent" because this person will control distributions from the Trust until your child is mature enough to make these decisions on her own. When possible, the Trustee should be someone other than the guardian (who is responsible for taking care of your child's physical, emotional, and spiritual needs) so that the system has checks and balances. The Trustee watches the guardian who, in turn, watches the Trustee. The Trustee choice is critical in a successful distribution of Trust funds.*
> *To download a free article on how to choose the right Trustee, visit:*
>
> **www.FamilyWealthMatters.com**

You and Alex named your best friend and Chelsea's godfather, Peter, to serve as trustee if Kaari was serving as Chelsea's guardian.

You initially figured you would name Kaari to be both the trustee and Chelsea's guardian, but Nat recommended that you name two different people to act as guardian and trustee, if possible.

The great news is that Kaari and Peter do not have to go through the court system to access your assets for Chelsea's benefit. Because of your smart planning, both your and Alex's $2-million estate tax coupons were used, meaning no estate tax is due.

As trustee, Peter is guided by Nat to work with Kaari as guardian and to determine Chelsea's financial needs, so that the money in the trust is used for its intended purpose: to care for Chelsea. Because you and Alex established the trust with clear directions that dictate its use, Kaari does not need to petition the court for access to the money. With the help of Nat, Kaari and Peter determine that Chelsea needs a full-time parent. Until Chelsea turns eighteen, Peter distributes money from the trusts so that Kaari can cover living expenses, allowing her to work part-time so that she can be available for Chelsea during this emotional time.

Later, when Chelsea turns eighteen, Peter will distribute money to Chelsea for college, transportation, a wedding, and other needs she may have.

With financial worries off of her chest, Kaari is able to take the time to find a part-time day job in nursing. While Chelsea is at school, Kaari works, continuing to move her career forward while still spending evenings with Chelsea, who, with the help of a grief counselor, is slowly but steadily regaining her stability.

Although it is not easy, when Chelsea graduates from high school, she feels strong enough to attend a university. Despite the rough patch following Alex's death, she scored high grades in high school. Between the grants and scholarships she received and the trust you and Alex set up for her, there are no limits on the money she can spend pursuing higher education.

The more guidance you can provide your chosen Trustee ("financial parent") about how you want Trust assets to be distributed to your child and/or their guardian, the better.

For most parents, this is hard to do because how do you even know where to start?

I'm going to make it easy for you.

Go to www.FamilyWealthMatters.com and download your free Trustee Distribution Guidelines worksheet. In this worksheet, I walk you through 10 different types of life events you may want to consider supporting for your child, such as travel, career choices, weddings, business, and transportation. Plus, I give you three possible guidelines you can give a Trustee; select one of the examples I provide or use the samples to spark ideas to create your own.

Nevertheless, perhaps because she lost both of her parents so young, Chelsea ends up marrying young and to an older man, a clinical researcher she met in one of the university's labs. Nick is a little showy, drives expensive cars, buys fancy suits, and flashes money to impress people. But he and Chelsea have similar interests, and Nick is a caring husband. He provides some structure and maturity in her life. Chelsea helps Nick in his business endeavors, and Nick helps Chelsea in her studies.

Because money is not an issue for Chelsea, she fails to discuss finances with Nick. But after graduating from college, Chelsea realizes several things about Nick. First of all, he has a mountain of debt and is up to his neck in credit card bills. He also lacks integrity in his business dealings. Unfortunately, within a few months of their marriage, Nick is sued because one of his biotech businesses was harvesting tissues without proper donor forms. Nick's own assets are reached by the judgment, but because Chelsea's assets belong to the trust, they are untouchable.

This experience, coupled with wisdom that comes with age, causes Chelsea to begin questioning her marriage to Nick. Chelsea wants to pursue a career of her own, Nick is not interested in having anything other than a stand-by-her-man wife. He wants to be with someone who will raise his children and support his career. Though Chelsea wants to do both of those things, she also wants to pursue her own independence.

Though she loves Nick, Chelsea wonders if she was rash in marrying Nick. After what seems like an endless stream of fights, Chelsea and Nick decide to divorce amicably. But the situation takes a twist when Nick tries to claim half of Chelsea's inheritance.

Chelsea's lawyer laughs when he hears the news. "Not a chance," Nat tells Nick. Nick's lawyer informs his client of the same. The money is protected by a trust, and Nick cannot touch it. Because her assets are held in trust, they cannot be reached by the divorce proceedings, and none will be distributed to her ex-husband as part of any dissolution settlement.

Chelsea is relieved to hear the news. Ready for a fresh start, Chelsea can use the money to start a business or attend graduate school, whatever her choosing. While her marriage definitely provided a setback in her life, Chelsea has the resources, education, and support network to move on and pursue her own dreams.

Turn to page 85.

ADDITIONAL RESOURCES:
For Choosing the Right Trustees and Making Smart Financial Choices

As parents, we have a myriad of financial decisions to make for our children: decisions that impact not only their future, but future generations as well.

It is your responsibility as a parent to leave behind sufficient financial resources for whoever will be caring for your child if you cannot. You can do this through savings or life insurance. For an article on what kind of life insurance and how much life insurance is right for your family, see www.FamilyWealthMatters.com.

The best way to make sure that your financial resources will be immediately available to your children or their guardian is to complete a Family Wealth Inventory and Assessment and become clear about what you have and what will happen to your assets if and when something happens to you.

You can do this during a Family Wealth Planning Session with a Personal Family Lawyer. Normally, a Family

Wealth Planning Session is $750. Readers of this book receive a free Family Wealth Planning Session by going to www.PersonalFamily-Lawyer.com and entering the unique code (WCU508) to receive a personal Family Wealth Planning Session absolutely free.

From the prior two stories, you now know how to protect your children's physical and financial well-being, but what about their emotional well-being? Turn to Story Three, where you will learn how to make decisions that will protect your children from any unnecessary emotional burden.

STORY THREE:
You and Aiko

Not a Lot of Assets, But a Whole Lot of Love

You and Aiko are not wealthy—at least not on paper. You both come from working-class families. You met at the state university, which you paid for by taking modest student loans and living frugally. While you were there, some of your college friends complained that you never joined them for ski trips and dinner out. But you never had to explain to Aiko, and Aiko was just as eager as you were to find free activities. Together, you attended outdoor concerts, hiked for miles, went to poetry readings at the local coffee shops, and listened to visiting speakers who came to the university. You and Aiko never had to pretend to be anything you were not, and it did not take long before you both knew you would always be each other's safe harbors.

With each other for support, you both obtained your degrees, quickly learning that college degrees do not equate to wealth. You always wanted to be a teacher, and Aiko approved, never suggesting that another profession might be more lucrative. In return, you gave Aiko your whole-hearted support to become a scuba instructor instead of taking a soul-sucking job in the business sector, even though Aiko did earn an MBA. Aiko loved animals and the environment, and the scuba position allowed Aiko to spend twenty hours a week volunteering at the local animal shelter and for the local chapter of the Sierra Club.

Twenty years later, you have three children. Your twins, Olivia and Colin, attend high school in your neighborhood. Your eighteen-year-old son, Jet, is in his freshman year of college at the same state university you and Aiko attended. You and Aiko were the first members of your respective families to attend college, and although your families were supportive, they would have been equally happy if you had made other, less costly choices. You and Aiko are determined to foster a new tradition: all of your children will attend college (even if they ultimately work as scuba instructors), and cost will be no obstacle for them.

Although you and Aiko still rent (who can afford to buy in Southern California?), you have managed to save about $150,000. In addition, you require your children to maintain good grades and take advantage of every extracurricular opportunity available. In that way, despite your modest incomes, you and Aiko hope to ensure that all three of your kids earn college degrees. Indeed, Jet is currently attending college on a full academic scholarship.

So while you might not be rich on paper, you and Aiko feel wealthier than you ever would have imagined as children. You thank the Powers that Be that you met Aiko. As the old saying goes, "Two times one is not two, but two thousand." Alone, you had been two kids from working-class families struggling to make it through college on shoestring budgets. Alone, you had only limited family support. Alone, you felt like outsiders when the other students left for their spring break vacations. Together, you have created a comfortable, cultured home, raised three happy kids who will all attend college, and managed to save $150,000 while doing work you loved. When you think about the potential for your children's future and for their children's future, you smile deep inside.

For Christmas, you and Aiko decide to drive the family to Northern California to visit your parents and ski. You are lucky that Jet, despite being in his first year at the university, is still interested in spending time with the family. You want to take the opportunity for one last family vacation before Jet drifts away, as most young adults do before coming back as men. A ski vacation will be perfect: something your kids have rarely experienced and a welcome change from your family's usual activities.

Unfortunately, because you have lived in sunny Southern California all your lives, you and Aiko are unfamiliar with the weather in Northern California and have little understanding of how dangerous highway driving can be in the wintertime. You notice dark skies after you pass into Northern California. At first, your only concern is whether you will have nice weather on the slopes. Neither of you recognizes the threat posed by the clouds amassing over the snow-packed highway.

When the snowstorm hits, it destroys visibility, making it impossible to see even a few feet ahead. The swirling snow blinds the road; in fact, you have no way to know whether you are still on the highway. You and Aiko want to pull over, but you are terrified of being hit by a similarly blinded driver behind you. Speaking in low murmurs, neither of you wants to let the kids realize how worried you are. Teeth clenched and hands white from gripping the steering wheel so hard, Aiko keeps driving, and together you press forward, trying to distinguish the road ahead. You are quickly exhausted, your backs ache, and your eyes start playing tricks on you from the strain. You want to cry, but pulling over seems as dangerous as continuing. You cannot remember the last time the kids said anything; despite your attempts to hide your worry, the kids are wide-eyed with concern.

And then, just like that, you drive out of the storm. The sky is still unremittingly gray, and the road is packed with snow, but at least you can see ahead. You breathe a collective sigh of relief and lean back in your seats. The kids start talking again. Aiko steps on the gas, and you do not object. The entire family is desperate to be done driving, out of the car, and checked into the lodge.

It happens without warning. As you cross a bridge packed with snow, your Southern California tires simply lose their grip on the snow-packed highway below. Fishtailing uncontrollably, the car leaves the highway just at the end of the guard rail and takes a nose dive to the ditch ten feet below.

You are unconscious, and later your children will learn that Aiko died instantly. Miraculously, none of the kids are seriously injured. Poor Jet is tested unfairly for his years, forced to leave you and the twins in the car while he searches for help or cell phone reception. Wearing his ski gear, he trudges down the snow-packed highway until he is able to flag a truck driver.

You and Aiko are airlifted to a hospital while your kids are taken by ambulance to the same hospital. The authorities ask Jet about any family members to call. He gives them your sister's name, and she is contacted and told to meet your children at the hospital.

Until your sister arrives, Jet must deal with the authorities, the doctors, and the twins. The police take statements. The hospital asks about health-care directives, medical records, and insurance. Jet is not sure what most of it means. He does not know what to do for his younger siblings, and he tries to maintain his composure until his aunt arrives or you awaken.

Your sister, Teresa, and her husband, Mitch, arrive the next afternoon. They too live in Southern California. When they arrive, the hospital informs them that you still have not regained consciousness and that your situation is critical. Mercifully, Teresa and Mitch relieve Jet's burden.

The hospital ombudsmen need to know about health insurance and health directives. The doctors need medical records in order to make competent decisions. The authorities need to know who will care for the twins, who are still minors. Your sister and her husband will do whatever is necessary to care for the children, but they feel too overwhelmed to make any immediate decisions. Everyone hopes you will regain consciousness and tell them what to do.

Finally, one of the ombudsmen prompts your sister gently. "Did they have wills? Or a trust? If so, a lot of the information we need might be found with those documents."

Do you and Aiko have wills? If so, turn to page 101. Or do you and Aiko have a trust? If so, turn to page 139.

You and Aiko Prepared Do-It-Yourself Wills

"Yes." Your sister smiles wearily in relief. She finally knows the answer to a question. "They have wills."

When the kids were young, you and Aiko prepared do-it-yourself wills, using a kit you found in a bookstore. Your family always lived frugally, and you and Aiko did not have money to hire expensive lawyers. Besides, you were both intelligent, resourceful people and you were used to caring for yourselves. You read everything you could about estate planning, discussed the issues extensively, and meticulously filled in the forms in your kit.

You both agreed that if one of you died, your assets would be transferred to each other. When both of you died, your assets would be divided evenly between your three children. The kit had detailed information about providing for guardians for your children, and you had both agreed on your sister, Teresa.

After completing all of the paperwork, you made copies of everything and gave them to Teresa and Mitch, to be opened in case of an emergency.

"We have copies at home," Teresa tells the ombudsman. She tries to reach her neighbors so that they can retrieve the documents and fax them to the hospital, but her neighbors are out of town for the holidays. The next day, she finally locates a friend who is able to drive to Teresa's house, locate the documents, and fax them to the hospital. At this point, you have been in the hospital for over forty-eight hours.

As soon as the documents arrive, Jet, Teresa, Mitch, and the hospital ombudsmen sit down to review them. Included are copies of both of your wills and health insurance information.

Thankfully, your wills clearly provide that your sister has legal authority to care for your minor children. Teresa and Mitch will face no problems assuming guardianship of Olivia and Colin while you are incapacitated.

But the more immediate question is how long that will be. How long will you remain unconscious at the hospital in Northern California, so far from home? You have plenty of health insurance, and you included all of this information in the packet you gave Teresa and Mitch. But to make important decisions for your care, the hospital needs copies of your medical records and any health care directives you have created. Without such information, the hospital does not know about any medical conditions or drug allergies you may have, any medications you are already on that might interact adversely with their treatments, or any limitations on life-saving measures you may have specified.

Did your documents contain health care directives? If not, turn to page 103. If so, turn to page 113.

Your Will Contains No Health Care Directives

You and Aiko drafted your wills with no expert assistance, using a do-it-yourself kit. You followed all of the directions and carefully discussed the issues you were directed to consider before meticulously completing the necessary paperwork. But you did not include health care directives, and even if you had, the directives would not have had the critical language needed in order to comply with the recent Health Insurance Portability and Accountability Act (HIPAA) regulations.

> Among other things, HIPAA regulates use and disclosure of health information. Intended to protect a person's privacy and keep medical information confidential, the federal law also hinders the transfer of critical information during emergencies. Due to stiff penalties for violations, medical professionals all but lock your medical records in an impenetrable vault.

Partly, the lack of forethought was because you thought in black and white; you assumed that either you would be dead or you would be functioning well enough to make your own decisions. An in-between scenario never occurred to you, perhaps because you and Aiko figured one of you would always be around to make decisions for the other. But the oversight was largely because the do-it-yourself kit you bought did not include health care directive instructions.

After realizing that you left no such directions, the hospital gently breaks the news to your family. Absent such directives, all decisions concerning your health care will fall on the shoulders of your eighteen-year-old son. It does not matter that your sister is better positioned to make such decisions; legally, the hospital must receive its instructions from Jet.

The lack of directives poses another problem. No one has any authorization to obtain your medical records, which are crucial to the hospital's ability to provide you with the appropriate care. To get them, the hospital must obtain authorization from Jet and complete arduous paperwork in order to comply with HIPAA, a well intentioned but often cumbersome congressional act meant, in part, to protect your privacy. Without HIPAA approval, the doctors must make their best guesses about your conditions and abstain from acting where the lack of knowledge could be dangerous.

Jet has only vague knowledge of your medical information. He tells the hospital administrative staff the name of your doctor, who is also Jet's doctor. Fortunately, Dr. Bowle treated you for all general health needs and is able to identify many of the specialists you saw. But although Jet, Teresa, the hospital, and Dr. Bowle all want the records transferred overnight, HIPAA interferes, and accessing the records takes time and red tape.

Despite the snail's pace, you still have not regained consciousness when the hospital finally gets Dr. Bowle's and your other providers' records. Maybe faster access to the records would have allowed more aggressive treatment early on and improved your chances. Maybe not. No one will ever know.

Either way, the doctors are unable to stem the bleeding in your brain. You suffer irreversible brain damage. They do not believe that you will ever regain consciousness. And even if you do, you will never have any meaningful cognitive function. You are being kept alive by machines, and the doctors believe you should be taken off life support. Ultimately, though, the choice will be left to your eighteen-year-old son.

Your family is devastated. Despite the doctors' warnings, they believed you would make a full recovery. Jet is being asked to make a decision that no one, especially not an eighteen-year-old, is prepared to make. Your family asks for time to make a decision.

Teresa is your older sister by six years. She has known you for your entire life. She knew you as a toddler, as a teenager, as a young adult, an adult, and as a parent and spouse. She knew you as a friend and a confidante. When you scraped your knees, got yelled at by your father, and had a fist fight with your best friend, she comforted you. She thinks she knows everything about you. In her heart, she knows you would not want to be kept on life support indefinitely. After much soul-searching, Teresa knows you would want your family to let you go.

Jet is eighteen. He has known you for his entire life. Every value, principle, and moral he holds came from you and Aiko. He thinks he knows everything about you. In his heart, he knows you would not want your family to give up. After much soul-searching, he knows you would want more time to fight.

Does either your sister or your eighteen-year-old son really know what you would want? You did not provide any specific directions. If you had, their disagreement never would have arisen, because your wishes would be the only ones that mattered.

Instead, for the next six months, you remain on life support while the situation between your sister and your son deteriorates. They both have the best of intentions. Your sister's heart breaks every time she sees you hooked up to all those machines, while the life slowly drains from your body even as your spirit is prevented from finding peace. She knows it is irrational and unfair, but part of her begins to hate Jet for what he is doing to you.

Jet feels angry, hurt, resentful, and guilty. He knows what Teresa thinks—and deep down, he wonders if she is right. At the same time, he could never, under any circumstances, be the one to make the decision to let you go. If you had planned ahead, he never would have been burdened with such responsibility. And even though he knows it is irrational and unfair, part of him begins to hate Teresa for the way her doubts make him feel. Because contact with her causes his own doubts to gnaw away at him, he avoids her.

You are never stable enough to be moved back to Southern California, so most of the time, you are alone. Teresa and Mitch take the twins home. They let your rental go, move the twins into their house, and put most of your belongings into storage for the time being. Jet returns to the university. They all try to drive north regularly to see you, but the drive is long, and everyone is struggling financially; taking time away from work and school is challenging, to say the least.

Teresa and Mitch are wonderful people; otherwise, you and Aiko would not have chosen them as your first-choice guardians. Yet they are not well-off. Mitch drives a delivery truck for a local beverage company, and Teresa works for a florist. Their own children are grown, and they have moved into a smaller home. They have no money set aside for two extra mouths. They do everything in their power to raise the twins in accordance with your wishes, but taking on two teenagers is a colossal burden.

Olivia and Colin both are involved in numerous extracurricular activities, all of which cost money. They are going through growth spurts and more than double the household consumption of food, not to mention energy and water costs. Olivia wears glasses, and Colin needs braces.

Even more importantly, Olivia and Colin need more than just financial support. They have just lost Aiko. You are in a permanently sedated condition in another city. They have been moved into a new home, a home that does not feel permanent, because they still believe you are going to regain consciousness. Their older brother is becoming increasingly hostile and withdrawn under the pressure that has been forced on him. Everything is strange, unfamiliar, and in limbo.

Teresa and Mitch would like to move into a bigger house so that some of your belongings can be brought out of storage. At least then, Olivia and Colin could have some familiar surroundings. They would like the twins to have their own rooms and a used car. They would like to fund some family activities for the twins and Jet. They would like Teresa to give up her weekend shifts at the shop so she can spend more time with the twins.

But they do not have the money to make all of these changes overnight. Instead of cutting back on their hours at work, they are forced to take on extra shifts until they can get their new budget ironed out.

They sure could use the $150,000 you and Aiko put away. But although you and Aiko named guardians for your children, you did not execute the necessary documents to allow someone to access your bank accounts in the event of your incapacity.

So your family must petition for a conservator to be appointed before any of them can access your money. Teresa and Jet are in the process of getting a court-appointed guardian to oversee financial matters during your incapacity. The process is long and expensive, and the court-appointed guardian will charge at least one hundred dollars an hour.

You would have preferred that your sister Teresa, the children's guardian, also be the guardian of your estate. But Teresa's weak credit and lack of assets prevent her from obtaining a bond, a necessary step to becoming an estate guardian unless expressly waived in writing, which was not explained in your do-it-yourself documents.

Besides, Jet mistrusts her and worries that any control she has over the estate might somehow be used to gain an upper hand in the battle over your continued treatment. Add this mistrust to the normal red tape, and every step in the process takes time and involves conflict. Until you have a guardian of your estate, no one in the family has any access to your and Aiko's assets. Though your insurance is covering your health care costs, neither your three children nor the guardian you chose to raise the twins can access a single penny of the money you and Aiko saved.

Turn to page 109.

Guardian of the Estate

Before the court can appoint a guardian, you die, and all the time spent petitioning to have an estate guardian appointed has been wasted. Instead, your estate will go through probate. Your will provides that your assets go in equal shares to your three kids. But when assets are disposed of via wills, the estate must go through probate, which is basically a lawsuit filed against your assets for the benefit of your creditors.

Probate is a system that the courts use to determine exactly how much of your assets should be divided among your creditors and how much should go to your family. The probate process takes at least one year in California and can be even longer—during which time your beneficiaries will have no access to your assets. Aggravating matters, your estate has to pay for a lawyer, court costs, appraisers, and other expenses.

So having already been deprived of your assets for six months—during which time your sister and her husband have taken on the burden of caring for you—your family must now wait another twelve to eighteen months to access your assets, which will be dissipated by probate fees. The irony is that you and Aiko did not have any creditors—a fact the court has no way of knowing until probate is complete.

At the completion of the probate, your $150,000 estate is $10,000 lighter. Jet receives one-third, close to $47,000, outright. You and Aiko raised him to understand that money does not bring happiness. But even if you had not, Jet would find no joy in his inheritance. Jet is in a dark place. Since your death, Teresa and Mitch have tried to reach out to him and encourage him to spend time with his younger siblings.

But Jet suffered all of the normal anguish of losing both parents at once, and he feels that your death was his fault. Away at the university and isolated by his conflict with Teresa, he does not know where to turn for help.

Instead, he immerses himself in music and painting, going hours without talking to anyone. He eats little and avoids his former friends. His paintings and music have grown increasingly full of despair and loneliness. When the inheritance check comes, he is physically repulsed. Without talking to anyone, he immediately writes two checks, each for one-half the amount of his inheritance: one to your favorite charity and one to the local humane society where Aiko worked. Teresa does not find out about this decision for some time.

Because the twins are minors, they cannot receive their inheritance until they turn eighteen. Instead, the court will hold onto their money until the twins reach adulthood. Teresa and Mitch can finally access the funds through the court-appointed guardian, who is assigned at the conclusion of the probate process, but the guardian does not agree to make distributions for luxuries like after-school activities or family vacations. Teresa and Mitch do get reimbursed for some of the money they spend on clothing and food, but not for any of their lost work time or the little things they bought in the hope of providing you comfort while in the hospital.

When the twins turn eighteen, they each receive about $45,000 outright.

They are both graduating from high school that year and are in the process of making decisions about college. Although they have suffered a terrible loss, including estrangement from their older brother, they have always had each other. They were lucky enough to stay in the same high school after the accident, so their friends have helped them through the ordeal. Their aunt and uncle made them feel like welcome additions in their home, shielding them from much of the conflict surrounding your medical decisions. Since you and Aiko had health insurance, the twins even were able to receive some counseling. In many ways, they are normal eighteen-year-olds.

And this is precisely the problem. Olivia and Colin are normal eighteen-year-olds who have just been handed $45,000 apiece. To them, this money seems like a million dollars. Even five thousand dollars, the amount they decide to give Teresa and Mitch, seems like a world of money. To them, five thousand dollars seems a generous payment. The twins are vaguely aware of the financial difficulty they have imposed on your sister and her husband, but because Teresa and Mitch tried to keep the twins from feeling any guilt, Olivia and Colin know very little about the actual cost incurred by their aunt and uncle. They do not know how much rent and groceries and utilities and car insurance cost.

They cannot imagine how their money could ever run out. They take loan and scholarship applications a little less seriously. As soon as he is installed in the dorms and away from the watchful eye of Teresa, Colin starts spending, buying clothes, books, CDs, expensive electronics, fancy cameras and phones, movies, and nights out.

Olivia, on the other hand, is interested in banking, and she decides to look into investment opportunities. She feels fortunate to meet Brian, a college student who befriends her instantly. Brian introduces her to an investment opportunity that promises to double her money in just a few months. Though Colin is distrustful of Brian, neither twin has the maturity or experience to recognize this "investment" for what it is: a scam.

Unbeknownst to both Olivia and Colin, the process of probate is public, and Brian "befriended" Olivia because he searched court records and found a target who would buy into his "investment" opportunity.

> *Want to read Jacqueline Lee Bouvier Kennedy Onassis's Will? How about the Last Will and Testament of Elvis Presley? Wills are public knowledge, which means that any unscrupulous person who wants to marry for money or prey on recent inheritors with investment schemes can easily determine who has inherited large chunks of money. (To download copies of these Wills, visit:* **www.FamilyWealthMatters.com***)*

By the end of their freshman year of college, both Colin's and Olivia's inheritances are gone. Colin squandered the money away, while Olivia was the victim of a predator.

Luckily, with the family's scant assets, the twins easily qualify for federally guaranteed student loans. They will graduate from college, but with over $25,000 in student loans each.

And what about your and Aiko's personal property? What becomes of that?

If you designated beneficiaries for your personal property, turn to page 129. If not, turn to page 133.

Your Documents Contain Health Care Directives

Thankfully, despite having created them yourselves without any expert help, you and Aiko included health care directives with the wills you prepared. As part of that process, you also executed HIPAA authorizations to allow your family to access your medical records and information. Your directives identified all of your providers, allergies, and major medical conditions. In addition to appointing Teresa as the guardian of your children, your directives granted Teresa with medical power of attorney and authorized her to obtain your medical records and make decisions for your health care. Your directives also provide with great specificity what sort of life-saving measures you want and under what circumstances you want to be taken off life support.

Among other things, HIPAA regulates use and disclosure of health information. Intended to protect a person's privacy and keep medical information confidential, the federal law also hinders the transfer of critical information during emergencies. Due to stiff penalties for violations, medical professionals all but lock your medical records in an impenetrable vault.

Teresa and her husband take charge immediately. Teresa is able to have all of your medical records faxed to the hospital within hours, and the hospital uses the information to make immediate and competent decisions about how to move forward with your treatment. Your children are never faced with the burden of making any medical decisions for you, even Jet, who is your closest living adult relative.

For the first week, your family members stay at a nearby hotel. At the end of the week, the doctors sit Teresa and Mitch down. Unable to stem the bleeding in your brain, the doctors fear that you have suffered irreversible brain damage. They do not believe you will ever regain consciousness. And even if you do, you will never have any meaningful cognitive function. Based on your directives, the doctors believe you should be taken off life support.

Teresa is devastated. Despite the doctors' warnings, she had hoped you would make a full recovery. She feels overwhelmed by the burdens that have been placed upon her. Three children are relying on her to tell them what to do next. Now the doctors are asking her to make a decision about your life. She asks them to give her twenty-four hours to make a decision.

Teresa is your older sister by six years. She has known you for your entire life. She knew you as a toddler, as a teenager, as a young adult, an adult, and as a parent and spouse. She knew you as a friend and a confidante. When you scraped your knees, got yelled at by your father, and had a fist fight with your best friend, she comforted you. She thinks she knows everything about you. In her heart, she believes that you would not want to be kept on life support indefinitely. After much soul-searching, she knows that you would want your family to let you go. Everything in your directives confirms what she believes.

The next day, she tells the doctors her decision.

Of your children, only Jet has any understanding that their aunt is involved in making such a decision. The twins are completely shielded. Jet knows more, but because the doctors, Teresa and Mitch, and your directives are all in agreement, he does not question the decision.

Teresa and Mitch arrange to have your bodies transported home so that the joint funeral can take place in your town. Teresa and Mitch take your kids home with them. After the funeral, they send Jet back to college. They let your rental go, move the twins into their house, and put most of your belongings into storage until everyone can go through them together.

Teresa and Mitch are wonderful people; otherwise, you and Aiko would not have chosen them as your first choice guardians. Yet they are not well off. Mitch drives a delivery truck for a local beverage company, and Teresa works for a florist. Their own children are grown, and they have moved into a smaller home. They have no money set aside for two extra mouths. They do everything in their power to raise the twins in accordance with your wishes, but taking on two teenagers is a colossal burden.

Olivia and Colin both are involved in numerous extracurricular activities, all of which cost money. They are going through growth spurts and more than double the household consumption of food, not to mention energy and water costs. Olivia wears glasses, and Colin needs braces. Even more importantly, Olivia and Colin need more than just financial support. They have just lost both their parents and moved into a new home. Many of their belongings and familiar surroundings are temporarily in storage. They feel disconnected from and alien to everything around them.

Teresa and Mitch would like to move into a bigger house, so that some of your belongings can be brought out of storage. At least then,

Olivia and Colin could have some familiar surroundings. They would like the twins to have their own rooms and a used car. They would like to fund some family activities for the twins and Jet. They would like Teresa to give up her weekend shifts at the shop so she can spend more time with the twins.

But they do not have the money to make all of these changes overnight. Instead of cutting back on their hours at work, they both take on extra shifts until they can get their new budget ironed out. They do the best they can. They make sure to reach out to Jet, even though he is technically an adult, doing everything within their power to keep Jet and his younger siblings in close contact.

They sure could use access to the $150,000 you and Aiko put away.

Your will provides that your assets will go in equal shares to your three kids. But when assets are disposed of via wills, the estate must go through probate, which is basically a lawsuit filed against your assets for the benefit of your creditors. Probate is a system that the courts use to determine exactly how much of your assets should be divided among your creditors and how much should go to your family. The probate process takes at least one year in California and can be even longer—during which time your beneficiaries will have no access to your assets. Aggravating matters, your estate has to pay for a lawyer, court costs, appraisers, and other expenses.

So having already been deprived of your assets for six months—during which time your sister and her husband have taken on the burden of caring for your youngest children—your family must now wait another twelve to eighteen months to access your assets, which will be dissipated by probate fees. The irony is that you and Aiko did not have any creditors—a fact the court has no way of knowing until probate is complete.

After eighteen months, your $150,000 has been reduced to about $140,000. Jet receives one-third, almost $47,000, outright. You and Aiko raised him to understand that money does not bring happiness. But even if you had not, Jet would find no joy in his inheritance. He contacts Teresa and Mitch and asks them to take the money and use it to care for the twins. Teresa and Mitch thank him profusely but tell him that they will open a savings account with the money, which Jet can access later. Jet assures them that he will never want the money, but Teresa and Mitch suspect this might change, knowing he can use the money for a down payment on a house or an emergency of his own. Not knowing much about money, Teresa and Mitch put the money in a regular savings account, earning a measly 2 percent interest rate.

Because the twins are minors, they cannot receive their inheritance until they turn eighteen. Instead, the court will hold onto their money until the twins reach adulthood. Teresa and Mitch finally can ask to access the funds through the court-appointed guardian who is assigned at the conclusion of the probate process, but the guardian does not agree to make distributions for luxuries like after-school activities or family vacations. Teresa and Mitch do get reimbursed for some of the money they spend on clothing and food, but not for any of their lost work time or ancillaries they bought in the hope of providing you comfort while you were hospitalized.

In your wills, you and Aiko named Teresa as the executor of your will. She would have been able to care for everything without a court-appointed guardian, and she would have been able to make decisions about how funds were spent for the benefit of the twins, but your wills did not waive the bond required for someone to become executor.

That means that Teresa has to qualify to be bonded (a bond is basically an insurance policy paid for by your estate in case the executor negligently squanders the estate), and because of her weak credit, she does not qualify.

This is not what you wanted, but your do-it-yourself kit did not mention the bond provisions.

Teresa and her husband, who have so generously cared for your twins for the past two years, never obtain access to any of the money you and Aiko set away. Desperate, and with his permission, they begin to access some of the money they had intended to hold onto for Jet.

When the twins turn eighteen, each receives about $45,000 outright.

Olivia and Colin are graduating from high school that year and are in the process of making decisions about college. Although they have suffered a terrible loss, they have always had each other. They were lucky enough to stay in the same high school after the accident, so their friends have helped them through the ordeal. Their aunt and uncle made them feel like welcome additions in their home. Since you and Aiko had health insurance, the twins even were able to receive some counseling. In many ways, they are normal eighteen-year-olds.

And this is precisely the problem. Olivia and Colin are normal eighteen-year-olds who have just been handed $45,000 apiece. To them, this money seems like a million dollars. Even five thousand dollars, the amount they decide to give Teresa and Mitch, seems like a world of money. To them, five thousand dollars seems a generous payment. The twins are vaguely aware of the financial difficulty they have imposed on your sister and her husband, but because Teresa and Mitch tried to keep the twins from feeling any guilt, Olivia and Colin know very little about the actual cost incurred by their aunt and uncle. They do not know how much rent and groceries and utilities and car insurance cost.

They cannot imagine how their money could ever run out. They take loan and scholarship applications a little less seriously. As soon as he is installed in the dorms and away from the watchful eye of Teresa, Colin starts spending, buying clothes, books, CDs, expensive electronics, fancy cameras and phones, movies, and nights out.

Olivia, on the other hand, is interested in banking, and she decides to look into investment opportunities. She feels fortunate to meet Brian, a college student who befriends her instantly. Brian introduces her to an investment opportunity that promises to double her money in just a few months. Though Colin is distrustful of Brian, neither twin has the maturity or experience to recognize this "investment" for what it is: a scam.

Want to read Jacqueline Lee Bouvier Kennedy Onassis's Will? How about the Last Will and Testament of Elvis Presley? Wills are public knowledge, which means that any unscrupulous person who wants to marry for money or prey on recent inheritors with investment schemes can easily determine who has inherited large chunks of money. (To download copies of these Wills, visit: **www.FamilyWealthMatters.com***)*

Unbeknownst to both Olivia and Colin, the process of probate is public, and Brian "befriended" Olivia because he searched court records and found a target who would buy into his "investment" opportunity.

By the end of their freshman year of college, both Colin's and Olivia's inheritances are gone. Colin squandered the money away, while Olivia was the victim of a predator.

Luckily, with the family's scant assets, the twins easily qualify for federally guaranteed student loans. They will graduate from college, but with over $25,000 in student loans each.

The twins, who were cared for so generously by their aunt and uncle, squander most of their money. Jet, who placed very little burden on his aunt and uncle, gave them his share because he was reluctant to use it. Never able to obtain the assistance they so desperately needed to help with the cost of caring for the twins, Teresa and Mitch reluctantly have accessed some of the money they intended to hold for Jet.

And what about your and Aiko's personal property? What becomes of that?

If you designated beneficiaries for your personal property, turn to page 121. If not, turn to page 125.

Your Will Designates Beneficiaries of Your Personal Property

About six months after the accident, while Jet is on break, your family gets together to go through your personal belongings.

While your family is very close, each of your children is a unique individual with different interests, different quirks, and different soft spots. Each inherited characteristics unique to you, and each inherited characteristics unique to Aiko. While you were alive, you loved seeing the melding that made you and Aiko such an unbreakable team.

Like Aiko, Jet loves animals. While the twins probably barely noticed them on the bookshelf, Jet loves the little menagerie of ceramic, glass, stone, wooden, and even plastic animals that Aiko amassed. Other people might have eventually thrown away the silly wind-up plastic frog and duck. Aiko never had been able to throw away an animal and had added every silly animal to the menagerie. The twins never commented on them, but Jet loved each of them since he was a baby, treasuring the additions as much as Aiko.

Olivia, on the other hand, loves all books. She jealously guards every book she has ever been given. Even as a toddler, she pretended to read your old college textbooks. She always asks for books for gifts, and if other family members are not careful, she hoards their neglected books in her own room. If you ever thought about taking any of your old books to Goodwill, Olivia wanted them for herself. Her room is lined with bookshelves, and she swears she has read every one of them.

Colin loves photography. He uses his allowance to buy photography books, and he loves the framed photographs you and Aiko used

to decorate your walls. None of the art is expensive, but Colin loves it all and wants to take pictures like that himself one day. He loves your Pentax LX, and when you were alive, he begged you to let him take pictures with it.

Because you thought about it ahead of time, you and Aiko specified, to the extent possible, who should receive all of your personal belongings. Jet gets first choice of anything animal related. Olivia gets first choice of any books, and Colin has dibs on photographic art and equipment. Your sister gets all of your kitchenware. Mitch gets the tools and lawn equipment. You left stories about a few items that were particularly important to you or that you received from your parents or grandparents. These special items are sure to become family heirlooms that will be handed on with loving care and stories from generation to generation.

Although it is bittersweet, your family is able to bond a little over their experience at the storage facility. They open boxes together and then check your will to see who is supposed to receive each item. They are able to share memories about you and Aiko related to your belongings. They remark upon particularly fitting designations. Some items are from your childhood and came to you through your parents. Teresa is able to share stories about your childhood with the kids, many of which they have never heard. Although several items are not designated for anyone, because each person thoughtfully has been given what mattered most, they are generous and honest with each other over the undesignated items. In the end, they all agree on boxes to be delivered to neighbors, other relatives, and local charities. They all feel a sense of catharsis from the day and feel closer as a family.

In the end, your family will be okay. But by not making all of your own choices in life, you left your children's futures vulnerable to poor choices by themselves and others. Are you completely satisfied with this outcome? If not, go back to page 95 and make different choices.

Your Will Did Not Designate Beneficiaries of Your Personal Property

About six months after the accident, while Jet is on break, your family gets together to go through your personal belongings.

While your family is very close, each of your children is a unique individual with different interests, different quirks, and different soft spots. Each inherited characteristics unique to you, and each inherited characteristics unique to Aiko. While you were alive, you loved seeing the melding that made you and Aiko such an unbreakable team.

Like Aiko, Jet loves animals. While the twins probably barely noticed them on the bookshelf, Jet loves the little menagerie of ceramic, glass, stone, wooden, and even plastic animals that Aiko amassed. Other people might have eventually thrown away the silly wind-up plastic frog and duck. Aiko never had been able to throw away an animal and had added every silly animal to the menagerie. The twins never commented on them, but Jet loved each of them since he was a baby, treasuring the additions as much as Aiko.

Olivia, on the other hand, loves all books. She jealously guards every book she has ever been given. Even as a toddler, she pretended to read your old college textbooks. She always asks for books for gifts, and if other family members are not careful, she hoards their neglected books in her own room. If you ever thought about taking any of your old books to Goodwill, Olivia wanted them for herself. Her room is lined with bookshelves, and she swears she has read every one of them.

Colin loves photography. He uses his allowance to buy photography books, and he loves the framed photographs you and Aiko used

to decorate your walls. None of the art is expensive, but Colin loves it all and wants to take pictures like that himself one day. He loves your Pentax LX, and when you were alive, he begged you to let him take pictures with it.

Unfortunately, you and Aiko did not think to specify beneficiaries for your personal property. If you had, you could have made sure that the important things went to the right people and that each child got those possessions that best reflected the qualities he or she had inherited from you both.

As it is, all of the kids are uncomfortable. They know that the purpose of the day is to divide your belongings between them. They know that you and Aiko rejected materialism and valued generosity. The concept of divvying up your possessions makes them feel guilty.

Teresa and Mitch sense the children's reticence but are unsure how to put the three kids at ease. They become unduly deferential themselves.

On the one hand, everyone wants to be polite and give everyone else a first choice. On the other hand, the children feel they are being insensitive if they do not want certain things. The children feel caught between showing too much interest in certain things and too little interest in others. Perversely, the more they want something, the more they feel they should let someone else have it. The more they do not want something, the more they feel they are disrespecting your memories if they turn it down.

Teresa, for her part, has sentimental connections to some of the items from your childhood or that came to you from your own parents. Teresa would like to claim some of those for herself, but she feels reluctant to speak up in front of your children, who are so clearly uneasy with this process. And Mitch recognizes the worth of some of the larger household goods. As the person most removed from the uncomfortable family dynamics around him, Mitch is the most able to make practical choices.

The first box contains books. Olivia has already co-opted so many of your books that she feels like she should give others a chance. She takes a few for herself. Jet and Colin are not that interested in most of the books, but they feel like they are supposed to take some anyway. Is it insensitive to turn down books that belonged to you and Aiko? Are they supposed to keep them for sentimental reasons? Unsure but completely unaware that anyone else genuinely might want these books, Jet and Colin each claim a handful.

A little later, the box with Aiko's menagerie is opened. Jet immediately breaks into tears and retreats. He wants them, but more than that, he wants Aiko. He wants not to have kept driving on that snowy day. He can barely talk. The others are unsure how to respond. They continue their stiff division of items, each taking a few pieces of the menagerie and setting a couple aside for Jet. It does not occur to him to protest.

When a box containing your photographic equipment is opened, Colin immediately offers it to everyone else. To him, it is the most valuable possession you owned, not for its dollar worth, but because he loved using it and he cherishes his memories of the time you spent together trying to take star shots and pictures of raindrops bouncing off leaves. Because Colin attributes such value to the equipment, he feels particularly compelled to be generous to the others. Mitch recognizes the dollar worth of the equipment, and when no one else seems to express any interest, he takes it.

In the end, everyone walks away with some important and sentimental pieces. The remainders are packed for neighbors with young children, other relatives, and your and Aiko's favorite charities. But what could have been a cathartic, bittersweet day of shared memories instead was an experience your family wants to forget. Their enjoyment of these items always will be slightly marred by the distinctly unpleasant and uncomfortable experience of rationing them to each other.

In the end, your family will be okay. But by failing to make clear all of your own choices in life, you left your hopes and wishes for the future vulnerable to poor choices by others. Are you completely satisfied with this outcome? If not, go back to page 95 and make different choices.

Your Will Designated Beneficiaries of Your Personal Property

About six months after the accident, while Jet is on break, your family gets together to go through your personal belongings.

While your family was very close, each of your children is a unique individual with different interests, different quirks, and different soft spots. Each inherited characteristics unique to you, and each inherited characteristics unique to Aiko. While you were alive, you loved seeing the melding that made you and Aiko such an unbreakable team.

Like Aiko, Jet loves animals. While the twins probably barely noticed them on the bookshelf, Jet loves the little menagerie of ceramic, glass, stone, wooden, and even plastic animals that Aiko amassed. Other people might have eventually thrown away the silly wind-up plastic frog and duck. Aiko never had been able to throw away an animal and had added every silly animal to the menagerie. The twins never commented on them, but Jet loved each of them since he was a baby, treasuring the additions as much as Aiko.

Olivia, on the other hand, loves all books. She jealously guards every book she has ever been given. Even as a toddler, she pretended to read your old college textbooks. She always asks for books for gifts, and if other family members are not careful, she hoards their neglected books in her own room. If you ever thought about taking any of your old books to Goodwill, Olivia wanted them for herself. Her room is lined with bookshelves, and she swears she has read every one of them.

Colin loves photography. He uses his allowance to buy photography books, and he loves the framed photographs you and Aiko used

to decorate your walls. None of the art is expensive, but Colin loves it all and wants to take pictures like that himself one day. He loves your Pentax LX, and when you were alive, he begged you to let him take pictures with it.

Although the do-it-yourself kit you and Aiko used had not prompted you to prepare health care directives, it had covered the importance of designating beneficiaries of your personal property. Jet gets first choice of anything animal related. Olivia gets first choice of any books, and Colin has dibs on photographic art and equipment. Your sister gets all of your kitchenware. Mitch gets the tools and lawn equipment.

Although it is bittersweet, your family is able to bond a little over their experience at the storage facility. They open boxes together and then check your will to see who is supposed to receive each item. They are able to share memories about you and Aiko related to your belongings. They remark upon particularly fitting designations. Although several items are not designated for anyone, because each person thoughtfully has been given what mattered most, they are generous and honest with each other with the undesignated items. In the end, they all agree on boxes to be delivered to neighbors, other relatives, and local charities.

They all feel a sense of catharsis from the day. Jet and the twins are able to bond over their shared memories and their common recognition of their parents' unique love for each of them. All of the distance the twins felt from Jet is forgotten. For Jet and Teresa, the day is a brief reprieve from their estrangement over Jet's choices for your medical care. While it may not make things better overnight, the experience plants seeds for a future reconciliation. Jet hears the love in Teresa's voice as she finds items from your childhoods and tells stories your children have never heard.

While Jet is in too dark a place to reconcile with Teresa right now, he will remember this day, and perhaps there is hope for the future.

Maybe your family will recover. But by not making clear all of your own choices in life, you left your wishes vulnerable to poor choices by others. Are you completely satisfied with this outcome? If not, go back to page 95 and make different choices.

Your Will Did Not Designate Beneficiaries of Your Personal Property

About six months after the accident, while Jet is on break, your family gets together to go through your personal belongings.

While your family was very close, each of your children is a unique individual with different interests, different quirks, and different soft spots. Each inherited characteristics unique to you, and each inherited characteristics unique to Aiko. While you were alive, you loved seeing the melding that made you and Aiko such an unbreakable team.

Like Aiko, Jet loves animals. While the twins probably barely noticed them on the bookshelf, Jet loves the little menagerie of ceramic, glass, stone, wooden, and even plastic animals that Aiko amassed. Other people might have eventually thrown away the silly wind-up plastic frog and duck. Aiko never had been able to throw away an animal and had added every silly animal to the menagerie. The twins never commented on them, but Jet loved each of them since he was a baby, treasuring the additions as much as Aiko.

Olivia, on the other hand, loves all books. She jealously guards every book she has ever been given. Even as a toddler, she pretended to read your old college textbooks. She always asks for books for gifts, and if other family members are not careful, she hoards their neglected books in her own room. If you ever thought about taking any of your old books to Goodwill, Olivia wanted them for herself. Her room is lined with bookshelves, and she swears she has read every one of them.

Colin loves photography. He uses his allowance to buy photography books, and he loves the framed photographs you and Aiko used

to decorate your walls. None of the art is expensive, but Colin loves it all and wants to take pictures like that himself one day. He loves your Pentax LX, and when you were alive, he begged you to let him take pictures with it.

Unfortunately, you and Aiko did not think to specify beneficiaries for your personal property. If you had, you could have made sure that the important things went to the right people—that each child got those possessions that best reflected the qualities he or she had inherited from you both.

As it is, the kids are uncomfortable. The distance between Jet and Teresa has grown, and the twins and Jet have been distant as a result. They know that the purpose of the day is to divide your belongings between them. They know that you and Aiko rejected materialism and valued generosity. The concept of divvying up your possessions makes them feel guilty.

Teresa and Mitch sense the children's reticence but are unsure how to put the three kids at ease. And they too are uncomfortable because of their recent conflict with Jet. So they become unduly deferential themselves.

On the one hand, everyone wants to be polite and give everyone else a first choice. On the other hand, the children feel they are being insensitive if they do not want certain things. The children feel caught between showing too much interest in certain things and too little interest in others. Perversely, the more they want something, the more they feel they should let someone else have it. The more they do not want something, the more they feel they are disrespecting your memories if they turn it down.

Teresa, for her part, has sentimental connections to some of the items from your childhood or that came to you from your own parents. Teresa would like to claim some of those for herself, but she feels reluctant to speak up in front of your children, who are so clearly uneasy with this process. And Mitch recognizes the worth of some of the larger household goods. As the person most removed from the uncomfortable family dynamics around him, Mitch is the most able to make practical choices.

The first box contains books. Olivia has already co-opted so many of your books that she feels like she should give others a chance. She takes a few for herself. Jet and Colin are not that interested in most of the books, but they feel like they are supposed to take some anyway. Is it insensitive to turn down books that belonged to you and Aiko? Are they supposed to keep them for sentimental reasons? Unsure but completely unaware that anyone else might genuinely want these books, Jet and Colin each claim a handful.

A little later, the box with Aiko's menagerie is opened. Jet immediately breaks into tears and retreats. He wants them, but more than that, he wants Aiko. He wants not to have kept driving that day. He wants not to have been the one to make medical decisions for you. He wants not to have isolated himself from the twins, and not to have fought with Teresa. He is so torn up that he cannot talk. The others, unsure how to respond, continue their stiff division of items, each taking a few pieces of the menagerie and setting a couple aside for Jet. Jet will never be the same.

When a box containing your photographic equipment is opened, Colin immediately offers it to everyone else. To him, it is the most valuable possession you owned, not for its dollar worth, but because he loved using it and he cherishes his memories of the time you spent together trying to take star shots and pictures of raindrops bouncing off leaves. Because Colin attributes such value to the equipment, he feels particularly compelled to be generous to the others. Mitch recognizes the dollar worth of the equipment, and when no one else seems to express any interest, he takes it, not because he is greedy, but because he does not want such a valuable piece of equipment to be donated to a stranger. Jet, who is suspicious of anything Teresa and Mitch do, misreads Mitch's intent. *He's out to get his greedy little hands on everything valuable*, Jet thinks as Mitch innocently piles the camera equipment on his pile.

And then the unthinkable happens. As Teresa stands to stretch, she accidentally steps on one of Aiko's glass animals, breaking it into three pieces. Jet has finally had enough.

He explodes. Hateful, vindictive, and hurtful words come flooding out of his mouth. He tells Teresa that he hates her. He accuses her of wanting you dead. Then he turns to Mitch and says, "Mom and Dad never liked you. They never thought you were good enough for Teresa. But they were wrong. The two of you greedy monsters are perfect for one another."

Of course, none of this is true. The twins, unsure of what to believe, try to quell the storm. This only makes Jet angrier. All of the pain Jet has felt turns to blind rage as he accuses Colin and Olivia of disrespecting your memory. Colin fights back tears, but Olivia, tired of her older brother's attitude, fights back.

"Don't blame us! You're the one who made the decisions! You're the reason the suffering lasted so long!" she screams.

Jet's face freezes. His baby sister has just confirmed his deepest fears. With Olivia, Colin, Mitch, and Teresa staring at him, Jet feels more alone than ever. Slowly, he picks up his belongings, turns, and leaves. No one stops him.

Your family will never be the same.

In silence, your sister, brother-in-law, and twin children pack the remaining items into boxes for neighbors, other relatives, and your and Aiko's favorite charities. In the end, everyone walks away with some important and sentimental pieces. But what could have been a cathartic, bittersweet day of shared memories instead was an experience your family wants to forget. Their enjoyment of these items always will be marred by Jet's outburst and the distinctly unpleasant and uncomfortable experience of rationing them to each other.

Your family has been battered by the tragedy of your death. By not making your own choices in life, you left your wishes and hopes for the future vulnerable to poor choices by others. Are you completely satisfied with this outcome? If not, go back to page 95 and make different choices.

You and Aiko Created a Trust.

"**Y**es." Your sister smiles wearily. She is happy to finally know the answer to a question. "They have a trust."

When your children were young, you and Aiko created an estate plan. Your family always lived frugally, and you and Aiko did not have money to hire expensive lawyers. You were both intelligent, resourceful people, and you were used to caring for yourselves, so you intended to create do-it-yourself wills using a kit from a bookstore. But in the end, you decided that your children's future was too important to handle informally, and you hired a lawyer with a flexible payment plan to ensure that you got the guidance you wanted.

It was worth every penny. You and Aiko at first thought the process would be simple. "We want our assets divided between our three children equally."

"What if they are still minors?" the Personal Family Lawyer asked. "Do you want your minor children to receive their inheritances outright, or would you rather they receive it at an age-appropriate time designated by you? Or even better, in a lifetime protected trust?"

"Isn't that for rich kids?" you and Aiko had asked, laughing a little in embarrassment at the size of your puny estate. The Personal Family Lawyer you met with explained that trusts used to be reserved solely for people with large assets but were being used more and more commonly by people who simply wanted to avoid probate, ensuring that their family had easy, immediate, and private access to the assets, and who wanted to protect their young children from unwise spending.

The Personal Family Lawyer explained, "A trust is just an agreement and set of instructions between the one who has the money to put into the trust—called the 'grantor,' 'trustor,' 'settlor,' or 'trustmaker'—and the trustee. The agreement is that the trustee will hold the property and follow the customized guidelines or instructions set out by you as the grantor for the benefit of the beneficiary."

The lawyer went on to say, "During your life, the trust creator—that's you—is the grantor, the trustee, and the beneficiary and has not given up control of any assets by putting them into the trust. Before your death, you determine who will serve as a successor trustee after your death, and you will decide who the beneficiaries will be."

Aiko had asked why a will was not sufficient, and your Personal Family Lawyer explained that if assets were passed through a will, the estate would have to go through a lengthy and costly court process that would prevent your family from reaching your assets at the time it needed them most: right after your death. And worst of all, the process is totally public, meaning any predator could find the names of the heirs to your estate.

"Probate" is the name of that court process. At the end of it, your assets and money are legally transferred to your heirs, but not until the court determines whether creditors have any claims to the estate. In addition to costing the estate about 5 percent of its worth, probate takes a minimum of twelve to eighteen months in California, and in some cases, it can be even longer.

On the other hand, explained your Personal Family Lawyer, if your assets are held in the trust, they would not be in your name and thus would not have to go through probate. That way, after your death, your children, beneficiaries, trustee, and guardian would be able to access your assets immediately without having to wait for and pay for the probate process. In addition, the trust assets and distributions would be totally private. No one but your children and their guardians would ever know how much your children inherited or when they would get it.

You and Aiko really loved knowing you could make everything as easy as possible for the people you loved. Making sure you were never a burden on anyone was one of your greatest values.

While Teresa and her husband, Mitch, were chosen as guardians of your minor children, in the event of your death, Aiko's cousin Janice was chosen as guardian of the estate. Janice was the person you trusted the most with financial responsibilities. Janice had good common sense and organizational skills. Though Janice was not a financial advisor, nor did she have extraordinary investment skills, you knew that Janice would hire a trusted advisor and seek guidance from your Personal Family Lawyer. You also knew that Janice would give the same answer you would when Olivia came to her at nineteen and said, "I want to drop out of college and start a business instead. I need $25,000."

Wherever possible, it is a good idea to name two separate people as guardian (responsible for your children's physical, emotional, and spiritual wellbeing) and Trustee (responsible for your estate's financial wellbeing). This keeps checks-and-balances in place whereby the Trustee and guardian watch over each other to ensure that they are both acting in the best interest of your children.

The Personal Family Lawyer talked to you about all kinds of issues you never would have thought of on your own. With your lawyer's guidance, you considered what would happen in the event of your death or incapacity while your children were still minors. Who would you want to make medical decisions for you if you were unable to make them for yourself? And what sort of guidelines you would want that person to follow? You compiled lists of your medical providers, conditions, and allergies and executed HIPAA authorizations so your family would be able to obtain your medical records, if needed.

When the hospital ombudsman asks if Teresa has access to your medical records, she knows exactly whom to call. Your Personal Family Lawyer faxes copies of everything to the hospital immediately, and the hospital receives copies of everything within minutes of Teresa's request. As soon as the documents arrive, Jet, your sister and her husband, and the hospital administration sit down to review them.

Thankfully, the documents clearly provide that your sister has legal authority to care for your minor children. Teresa and Mitch will have no problems assuming legal guardianship while you are incapacitated.

The more immediate question is how long you will be incapacitated. How long will you remain unconscious at the hospital, so far from home? You have plenty of health insurance, and you included all of that information in the packet you gave Teresa and Mitch. But in order to make important decisions for your care, the hospital needs copies of your medical records and any health care directives you have created. Without such information, the hospital does not know about any medical conditions or drug allergies you may have, any medications you are already on that might interact adversely with their treatments, or any limitations on life-saving measures you may have specified.

Thankfully, because you and Aiko had deviated from your usual do-it-yourself routine, you have signed health care directives and executed HIPAA authorizations that allow your family to access your medical records and information. Your directives identified all of your providers, allergies, and major medical conditions. In addition to appointing Teresa as the guardian of your children, your directives granted Teresa medical power of attorney and authorized her to obtain your medical records and make decisions for your health care. Your directives also provided, with great specificity, what sort of life-saving measures you want and under what circumstances you would want to be taken off life support.

Teresa and her husband take charge immediately, and the hospital is able to use your medical records to make immediate and competent decisions about how to move forward with your treatment. Your children, including Jet, your closest living adult relative, are never faced with the burden of making any medical decisions for you.

For the first week, your family members stay at a nearby hotel. At the end of the week, the doctors sit Teresa and Mitch down. Unable to stem the bleeding in your brain, the doctors fear that you have suffered irreversible brain damage. They do not believe that you will ever regain consciousness. And even if you do, you will never have any meaningful cognitive function. Based on your directives, the doctors believe you should be taken off life support.

Teresa is devastated. Despite the doctors' warnings, she had hoped you would make a full recovery. She feels overwhelmed by the burdens that have been placed upon her. Three children are relying on her to tell them what to do next. Now the doctors are asking her to make a decision about your life. She asks them to give her twenty-four hours to make a decision.

Teresa is your older sister by six years. She has known you for your entire life. She knew you as a toddler, as a teenager, as a young adult, an adult, and as a parent and spouse. She knew you as a friend and a confidante. When you scraped your knees, got yelled at by your father, and had a fist fight with your best friend, she comforted you. She thinks she knows everything about you. In her heart, she believes that you would not want to be kept on life support indefinitely. After much soul-searching, she knows that you would want your family to let you go. Everything in your directives confirms what she believes.

The next day, she tells the doctors her decision.

Of your children, only Jet has any understanding that their aunt is involved in making such a decision. The twins are completely shielded. Jet knows more, but because the doctors, Teresa and Mitch, and your directives are all in agreement, he does not question the decision.

Teresa and Mitch arrange to have your bodies transported home so that the joint funeral can take place in your town. Teresa and Mitch take your kids home with them. After the funeral, they send Jet back to college. They let your rental go, move the twins into their house, and put most of your belongings into storage until everyone can go through them together.

Teresa and Mitch are wonderful people; otherwise, you and Aiko would not have chosen them as your first choice guardians. Yet they are not well-off. Mitch drives a delivery truck for a local beverage company, and Teresa works for a florist. Their own children are grown, and they have moved into a smaller home. They have no money set aside for two extra mouths. They do everything in their power to raise the twins in accordance with your wishes, but taking on two teenagers is a colossal burden.

Olivia and Colin are both involved in numerous extracurricular activities, all of which cost money. They are going through growth spurts and more than double the household consumption of food, not to mention energy and water costs. Olivia wears glasses, and Colin needs braces. Even more importantly, Olivia and Colin need more than just financial support. They have just lost both their parents and moved into a new home. Many of their belongings and familiar surroundings are temporarily in storage. They feel disconnected from and alien to everything around them.

Teresa and Mitch would like to move into a bigger house, so that some of your belongings can be brought out of storage. At least then, Olivia and Colin could have some familiar surroundings. They would like the twins to have their own rooms and a used car. They would like to fund some family activities for the twins and Jet. They would like Teresa to give up her weekend shifts at the shop so she can spend more time with the twins.

Thank goodness you and Aiko splurged on a Personal Family Lawyer! Almost immediately after your death, Teresa and Mitch can access the money in the trust to meet your kids' needs, including grief counseling. The estate does not go through probate, a time-intensive and costly process that can freeze funds for twelve to eighteen months. And everything happens in the privacy of your Personal Family Lawyer's office. Your Personal Family Lawyer guides Janice and Teresa with kindness and understanding throughout the whole process.

The money in the trust is administered and supervised by Janice, who simply ensures that the money is used for its intended purpose: to care for your children. Teresa and Mitch do not need to petition the court for access to the money, but need only submit requests to Janice. If it comes down to it, and they can show Janice that the twins need a full-time parent, Teresa will be able to obtain money from the trust so that she can stay home until the twins turn eighteen. Once they do, the twins will be able to obtain funds directly from the trustee, as Jet already does. Janice shares your financial values, and she must approve all trust distributions until the kids turn thirty, at which point if there is anything left, they will take over control.

Your estate is not huge and will not last forever, but the money has been put into safe investments to earn a 5 percent or greater return. No one will get rich from your estate, but Teresa and Mitch are freed from the additional financial burden of your twins, and Jet can continue with college.

Additionally, your trust specifies that the twins must go to college if they are to receive any additional access to trust assets once they turn eighteen. In this way, you have ensured that despite your and Aiko's modest assets, all three of your children will graduate from college. Your and Aiko's dream of starting a new tradition, in which all family members graduate from college, will be a reality despite your deaths.

About six months after the accident, while Jet is on break, your family gets together to go through your personal belongings.

While your family is very close, each of your children is a unique individual with different interests, different quirks, and different soft spots. Each inherited characteristics unique to you, and each inherited characteristics unique to Aiko. While you were alive, you loved seeing the melding that made you and Aiko such an unbreakable team.

Like Aiko, Jet loves animals. While the twins probably barely noticed them on the bookshelf, Jet loves the little menagerie of ceramic, glass, stone, wooden, and even plastic animals that Aiko amassed.

Other people might have eventually thrown away the silly wind-up plastic frog and duck. Aiko never had been able to throw away an animal and had added every silly animal to the menagerie. The twins never commented on them, but Jet loved each of them since he was a baby, treasuring the additions as much as Aiko.

Olivia, on the other hand, loves all books. She jealously guards every book she has ever been given. Even as a toddler, she pretended to read your old college textbooks. She always asks for books for gifts, and if other family members are not careful, she hoards their neglected books in her own room. If you ever thought about taking any of your old books to Goodwill, Olivia wanted them for herself. Her room is lined with bookshelves, and she swears she has read every one of them.

Colin loves photography. He uses his allowance to buy photography books, and he loves the framed photographs you and Aiko used to decorate your walls. None of the art is expensive, but Colin loves it all and wants to take pictures like that himself one day. He loves your Pentax LX, and when you were alive, he begged you to let him take pictures with it.

Because you thought about it ahead of time, you and Aiko specified, to the extent possible, who should receive all of your personal belongings. Jet gets first choice of anything animal related. Olivia gets first choice of any books, and Colin has dibs on photographic art and equipment. Your sister gets all of your kitchenware. Mitch gets the tools and lawn equipment.

Although it is bittersweet, your family is able to bond a little over their experience at the storage facility. They open boxes together and then check your will to see who is supposed to receive each item. They are able to share memories about you and Aiko related to your belongings. They remark upon particularly fitting designations. Some items are from your childhood and came to you through your parents. Teresa is able to share stories about your childhood with the kids, many of which they have never heard. Although several items are not designated for anyone, because each person thoughtfully has been given what mattered most, they are generous and honest with each other over the undesignated items. In the end, they all agree on boxes to be delivered to neighbors, other relatives, and local charities. They all feel a sense of catharsis from the day and feel closer as a family.

The last thing they do before going to bed that night is to listen to the CD you recorded many, many years before, when you met with your Personal Family Lawyer to plan for your life and your legacy. They heard you and Aiko talk about the life lessons you hoped to pass on and the love you felt for all of them. Despite their despair at losing you, your children feel infinite peace and inner knowledge that everything will work out as it is supposed to, and they feel the loving embrace of an energy greater than themselves.

Congratulations. Your choice to plan for your life and your legacy had the lasting impact of increasing your whole family wealth for generations to come. You have left the world a better place. Turn to page 149 for more resources on creating a lasting family legacy.

ADDITIONAL RESOURCES:
Making Life as Easy as Possible for Your Loved Ones, Even if You Don't Have a Lot

*R*egardless of the size of your assets, you want to make sure that your financial resources will be available immediately to your children and/or their guardian. The best way to do that is to complete a Family Wealth Inventory and Assessment worksheet and find clarity about what you have and what will happen to your assets if and when something happens to you.

You can do this during a Family Wealth Planning Session with a Personal Family Lawyer. Normally, a Family Wealth Planning Session is $750. Readers of this book receive a free Family Wealth Planning Session by going to www.PersonalFamilyLawyer.com and entering the unique code (WCU508).

If you do not have any assets, you still must have documents that give permission and instructions to the people you choose to make your health care decisions if you cannot. In addition, you must provide documentation granting these people the power to access your bank accounts and make legal decisions for you.

These documents are known as "health care directives" or "living wills and durable powers of attorney." If you choose not to work with an attorney, visit www.FamilyWealthMatters.com for a list of resources and to download free or low-cost form documents. Though these documents are not as good as documents prepared specifically for you and your family, they are better than nothing at all.

You will also want to make sure that your personal belongings are distributed in a way that will not cause even more pain for your family. The more you can specify in advance, the better. Go to www.FamilyWealthMatters.com to download a free Personal Property Memorandum for your use.

ABOUT
the Author

A lexis Martin Neely is a nationally recognized authority, author, and speaker on family and estate planning. Recognized by *Worth* as one of the country's top one hundred lawyers, Alexis is founder of Martin Neely & Associates, an estate planning law office in Southern California, as well as the Family Wealth Planning Institute, a nationwide cadre of Personal Family Lawyers who are specifically trained to help parents prepare their kids for life without them.

Alexis graduated first in her law school class from Georgetown University Law Center and continues to receive acclaim. For the past three years, *Los Angeles Magazine* has recognized Alexis as a Rising Star, an award bestowed upon the top attorneys under the age of forty.

She is the creator of www.KidsProtectionPlan.com, a free website that guides parents through a three-step process to help them decide who should be named guardians for their kids, teaches them the six common mistakes many parents make, and allows them to legally document their choices absolutely free. Her articles have been published in *Healthy Wealthy nWise*, Hot-MomsClub.com, and *Ladies Who Launch*. She has been featured on many radio programs, National Public Radio, *The Money Answers Show*, and Better TV. Alexis is often quoted by the *Wall Street Journal* and *Lawyers Weekly*.

Most importantly, Alexis is driven by her vision of preparing her own kids, Kaia and Noah, for lives of wealth, health, and happiness.

Free Teleseminar for Moms Only Reveals How to Protect Your Family, Secure Your Wealth and Take Charge of Your Future"

20% of elderly women are entering poverty in their 70s and 80s due to poor choices made without information. The time for you to take action is now!

Here are 7 reasons why you should reserve your spot today...

1. ...You'll learn how to make sure your **children's future is not left in the hands of a broken down court system** and a Judge who doesn't know you or your kids.

2. ...You'll discover how to **legally keep your family wealth in your pocket and out of the government's.**

3. ...You'll hear the secrets that guarantee you won't become one of the 20% of elderly women living in poverty ... **the time to secure your future is NOW!**

4. ...**You'll discover how to pass on your family's WHOLE WEALTH** not just your money...Make sure your children are raised with **your values, stories, insights and experiences.**

5. ...You'll discover exactly how to **take control of your finances if something should happen to your spouse.**

6. ...You'll discover **whether your family is at risk to pay unnecessary estate taxes.**

7. ... You'll discover how you can **protect your kids' inheritance** from a divorce or a lawsuit.

This FREE Teleseminar for MOMS ONLY will show you how to **get your financial house in order, take control of your finances** and **secure your children's future.**

www.MomsFreeCall.com

What Will Happen to Your Kids?
Your Money? Your Business?
Your House? Your Life Insurance?
Who Will Your Loved Ones Turn To?

Get all the answers you need during a Family Wealth Planning Session with a Personal Family Lawyer!

Before your Family Wealth Planning Session, you will complete a Family Wealth Inventory and Assessment and start the process of getting your financial house in order.

During your Family Wealth Planning Session, you will discover what would happen under your current plan (or the plan the State has for you) and be empowered to design a plan to ensure things happen the way you want them to and as easily as possible.

After your Family Wealth Planning Session, you'll be surprised at how painless and easy the whole process was for you and your family and you will sigh with relief knowing everything is taken care of throughout your life and beyond.

If You Own Your Own Home or Have Money in the Bank, Give Your Family This Gift and Request a Family Wealth Planning Session Today!

A Family Wealth Planning Session With a Personal Family Lawyer is Normally $750. As a Bonus for Purchasers of Wear Clean Underwear, Use Code WCU508 and Your Family Wealth Planning Session is Free Plus Receive over $300 In FREE BONUS audio gifts!

Go to www.PersonalFamilyLawyer.com or
Call 866-999-3974 and Use Code WCU508

PERSONAL FAMILY LAWYER
your lawyer for life

Free Family Wealth Building
Tips For Your Family!

www.FamilyWealthMatters.com

Here's a Taste of What You'll Get By Subscribing:

❖ How to GUARANTEE your children are raised with your values, insights, stories and experience

❖ How to prepare your children to lead lives of PASSION and PUR-POSE and GET WEALTHY doing it

❖ How to put the passage of your wealth on AUTO-PILOT and make life easy for the people you love most

❖ How to capture the 75% of wealth most often lost between generations... this WILL make and keep your family RICH!

It's completely FREE, and you may
unsubscribe at any time

www.FamilyWealthMatters.com

Family Wealth
PLANNING INSTITUTE

CPSIA information can be obtained
at www.ICGtesting.com
Printed in the USA
JSHW032139290920
8320JS00001B/2

9 781600 374418